AF531814

The Idea of a University: Jamia Millia Islamia
Rakhshanda Jalil (Editor)

First Published, 2009

ISBN 978-81-89833-95-4

Published by
AAKAR BOOKS
28 E Pocket IV, Mayur Vihar Phase I, Delhi-110 091
Phone : 011-2279 5505 Telefax : 011-2279 5641
aakarbooks@gmail.com; www.aakarbooks.com

Printed at
Arpitprintographers, Delhi 110 032
arpitprinto@yahoo.com

EDITORIAL

The present volume is a collection of articles written shortly after the encounter between the Special Branch of Delhi Police and a group of suspected terrorists in Batla House, in the neighborhood of Jamia Millia Islamia. Some are written by members of the Jamia *biradari*; others by those who are from the big world outside Jamia. Some contributors are teachers and academics, others are writers and thinkers. Some contributions are short, intuitive pieces, others longer, more insightful essays. Some make deeply personal observations about living and working in Jamia, others speak with fondness and regard for the institution and all it stands for. Most were written in the critical days immediately after the encounter; they are the ones that speak from the heart. Almost all, irrespective of their tone and tenor, are emphatic assertions of the 'idea' of Jamia – an idea that is in consonance with plural nationhood and composite culture.

We felt the need to preserve these diverse writings by securing them between the covers of a book for two reasons. One, the September encounter is not over as far as this University is concerned; its effects are still being felt. It is taking us a long time to rub away the tar that has been painted on us for no fault of ours. That random incidents which happened in our vicinity should erase all that we have achieved and all that we have stood for in the eight decades of our existence is a cause of real concern for all of us at the Jamia. The other reason to anthologize these scattered pieces was the composite, coherent, clear picture that emerges from within these pages. Reading them together, we were struck by the common thread that runs through them. Equally, we were struck by the composite picture that emerges from these pages. It is this picture that we wish to share with a larger readership.

Some of you may be familiar with Jamia's unique place in the history of this country but for those who are not it may be worthwhile to, briefly, re-visit the legacy of this somewhat unusual institution. The fanfare with which universities in British India were usually started was entirely missing in the case of Jamia Millia Islamia. A splinter group of ardent nationalists lead by Maulana Mohamed Ali broke away from the MAO College at Aligarh to set up a new kind of educational institution. Devoted to the service of the nation, it was bent upon shaping young men and women into citizens of a modern vibrant India. And so, on 29 October 1920, the Jamia Millia Islamia came into being. Its commitment to plural nationhood and composite culture meant, from early on, that it was determined to plough its own furrow and chart its own destiny. The lamp of *nai taleem* burnt brightly here and teachers like Dr Zakir Husain, Abid Husain, Mohammad Mujeeb and others worked tirelessly to usher in a new system of imparting education.

Education, *ilm,* and faith, *deen,* had been the twin engines that had propelled Jamia in its early days. Its founders wanted to colour faith with the many-splendoured hues of education, and *vice versa.* But to achieve this they insisted on meeting a basic condition – to view faith not in a narrow, bigoted sense but help create an ambience that would be conducive for comprehending real belief in its truest, widest, highest sense. In this way, they were able to contribute to what Mohammad Mujeeb, one of its vice chancellors, memorably put it: 'the outlook or *weltanschaung*, the recognition of the thought, the values, and the cultures of so many peoples of the world.' This, Mujeeb firmly believed, was Jamia's chief contribution to the making of a secular India.

In the early days, the Jamia was taken to be little more than an idealistic venture destined to die an early death from natural causes, chiefly the want of enough men of conviction and sufficient funds to see them through. But like all ideas whose time has come, the Jamia refused to die. Against all odds, it simply grew – sometimes in spurts and gushes, sometimes through prolonged processes of slow maturation. Money too came in fits and starts and whenever it needed them the most, the Jamia found enough committed men and women to nurture its special qualities. From a handful of tents in Aligarh to the sprawling 210-acre campus in South Delhi, the Jamia has indeed come a long way. From its first proper home in a bungalow in Aligarh's Badar Bagh, to a bustling complex of schools, faculties and institutions, it has been a long journey. For very long the Jamia chose to live in a shell of its own making, hide its light under a bushel, keep its experiments in the field of education and culture to itself and generally allow the world to view it as a curiosity, a whimsical, other-worldly sort of place, a retreat from the mainstream. Its quaintness drew the occasional high-minded visitors who sought 'otherness' or an alternative to the mainstream but kept away the serious student and the professional scholar.

But recent years have seen many changes. Robust growth and generous funding have not merely brought about physical changes in the university, but also ushered in many changes in the composition of its faculty and students. Today, Jamia draws staff and students from a wider swathe than ever before. It boasts of thirty-eight Departments spread over nine Faculties. Twenty seven specialized research centers have been established, of which many have come up in the past four years alone. There are 12,000 students, 735 academic staff and 1,108 non-teaching staff. There are 1,000 seats for boys, 415 for girls and 90 for working women in the various halls of residence on the campus. Its size works wonderfully in its favour as does its location. By virtue of being located in Delhi, it enjoys a distinct cosmopolitanism. Its campus is co-educational and gender-friendly.

While the Jamia continues to be difficult to describe or define, it is no longer a recalcitrant child bent upon being odd and different from others. This 'lusty child of the freedom struggle' as it was once memorably called, has grown up to become a modern, bustling, vibrant university. But it is a university with a singular difference. It has a past that sets it apart from other educational institutions. More importantly, it has a legacy of intellectual curiosity, of engagement with the community in which it is situated and of looking for ways and means in which to forge creative syntheses between the modern and the traditional. Given its rich inheritance and vigorous growth, it seemed a shame that the changes in public perception were slow in coming and full of misgivings and misinterpretations at best. For many in India and abroad, the Jamia was a largish *madarsa* at best, a destination by default and not always of first choice. In Delhi at least, those who did not make it to Delhi University, then looked around at other options and settled, rather grudgingly, for the Jamia.

While within the university, there was little doubt or confusion over its identity, the outside world either continued to turn a blind eye towards it or dismissed it as a bit of an anachronism. Those who visited its campus were struck by the changes wrought by recent years of prosperity; most however took these changes to be merely cosmetic, that is, amounting to little more than new buildings, gates and parks, signs of money well spent but amounting to little else. Those who had never been to the Jamia, of course, continued to think of it as an old world institution, a curiosity, a relic left-over from an idealistic past when the words secular and nationalist could be spoken in the same breath and understood to have some meaning. Clearly, neither perception was true. Equally clearly, the time had come for the Jamia to, if not beat its own drum, at least safeguard its own interests. It had to not merely suitably alter its public perception; it had to, far more importantly, take charge of how it was perceived. In other words, not only would it need to carve out a distinct profile for itself, one that was true to its present self and not a stereotype perpetuated by popular misperception, but also put in place ways and means whereby this profile could be accurately read by sufficiently large numbers of people.

The university therefore set itself two measurable objectives: one, to be in the news; and two, to stay in the news. For the Jamia no news is good news was a thing of the past. It had to now aggressively position itself in the media. The days of staying out of the news to stay out of trouble and keep a low profile were gone. Gone also was the role of the University PRO, or Public Relations Officer, who swung into action only to do damage control, down play issues related to union trouble or clashes within groups of students and generally ward off bad press but make no effort to woo let alone seek public attention. Increasingly, it began to be felt that there was nothing to be gained by undue modesty. A great deal was happening in the university, all of which was of interest to a large body of people, both academic and non-academic. And so whether it was a new digitization programme at the university archive or the issuance of electronic library cards, a new language laboratory or the introduction of a new super-specialisation, the naming of a new park or the installation of an IT centre, better facilities for those with special needs or the upgradation of its hostel rooms, what happened within the university, it was felt, was of interest to those outside it. Things that had so far been considered not news-worthy were not only being positioned in the media, but were actually being lapped up by the discerning public.

Remember, that for far too long the Jamia had been far too diffident and self-effacive. It took courage to assume that the world outside its campus was interested in its new installations and improvisations. Somehow it found the necessary courage, got over its inhibitions and began to shed some of the layers of opacity that hid it from the world. But a stray mention in the newspapers was not going to take it very far. Public interest is notoriously short; public memory even shorter. Moreover, every time a stray accident happened in the neighbourhood, the University became the target. Jamia hit the headlines for the wrong reasons and more often than not those wrong reasons tended to linger in popular perception. A pedestrian mowed down by a bus in the Jamia vicinity made headlines with the implied sub-text that the neighbourhood was unsafe, even unruly. As it turned out, the events of 19 September 2008 proved our worst apprehensions.

Something had to be done whereby a healthy, right-minded interest could be instilled, and more importantly, sustained. Better still, whereby the university and the community (here I use the word not in a narrow parochial way but in its broadest sense to mean society at large) could enter into a partnership where both would benefit. The Jamia had to not just make news to stay in the news it had to do so in a manner that was in keeping with its secular, syncretic, pluralistic legacy. What better way than by promoting culture, that too a culture that was not the *virasat* or legacy of some, but culture that could be shared and understood both within the Jamia *biradari* and outside.

In the West, art and culture have for very long been an extremely important part of academic life on campuses. Cultural activities are, in fact, so fully integrated in the educational system that they cease to be seen as extra-curricular. Culture and its many off-shoots are viewed as co-curricular activities in the developed world. The word 'co-curricular' itself was coined to present a holistic and integrated approach to creative activities on campuses. In the process, the university system became 'sites' for creative expression and universities produced not just plays, publishing and entertainment troupes but also fostered poets, musicians, painters, and a host of others. The link-up between the artist and the student, the cultural event and a ready audience was so entirely uncontrived that it never seemed to be assiduously created. It just was there and it was taken for granted. The debate between extra and co-curricular activities was settled a long time ago.

In India, on the other hand, we have maintained a distinction between the two. So much so that the expression *padhoge likhoge banoge nawab, kheloge koodoge to hoge kharab* reflected a certain mindset. The vast majority of Indian educational institutions have in-built mechanisms to stifle creative energy and most continue to make a distinction between creative pursuits and curriculum-based learning. Moreover, cultural programming and the promotion of culture is, in India, traditionally seen as the prerogative of institutions and academies devoted to the task, or set up by the government with the specific aim of promoting culture. We in the jamia chose to differ. We decided that creating an ambience in which our students could be sensitized about the important role they perform in society is just as vital as the education we impart.

We believed universities are far better placed to position and promote culture since unlike the *parishads* and the *anjumans* they do not preach to the converted but are more likely to have fresh, lively, and relatively un-jaded audiences. We were convinced that a space had to be created for culture – for our own students but one that would be open to the public as well.

And so we set out with zeal and earnestness to unleash a cultural blitz upon our campus. There was, of course, a quantum jump in the number of academic programmes such as seminars, symposia, conferences and workshops organized in comparison to previous years but this was not enough, for these were either too specialized or too esoteric or tailored for only a certain number of participants. We needed to do something bigger, something that involved large numbers of people, something that had the potential to draw audiences from across the city to our campus, even if it meant venturing into areas that are, strictly speaking, non-academic. We began to steadfastly organize *kitab melas*, film screenings, concerts, public performances, street plays, poetry readings. We began to seize the topical and the contemporary, culling and 'using' what was in keeping with our liberal, multi-cultural, multi-lingual, multi-ethnic tastes. Occasionally, we chose to be arbiters of good taste, bucking the trend and introducing new motifs in existing debates. For example, we were the first to initiate an introspection on the Progressive Writers' Movement causing many other literary institutions to hold seminars and symposia on the subject in our wake. When the Tsunami struck South India in 2004, we organized musical concerts to raise over Rs 14 lakh for the Prime Minister's Relief Fund. We hosted a 50-member delegation from Pakistan during a festival called "Pen for Peace" giving a new dimension to Track Two Diplomacy. All this was our way of sensitizing our students on vital issues that slip through the cracks of public perception as well as fulfill the cultural needs of the varied student body and at the same time draw attention to our self. This was our way of saying: Come and see us, get to know us. We can't give jobs or admissions to all but our programmes are free and open for everyone. We may be small and different compared to the collossus up north, but we have arrived and we mean to stay.

Four years ago Jamia had crafted a pivot of engagement with the community, the *mohalla-abadi*, amidst which it is situated. This was the Outreach Programme. Imbued with Nehruvian idealism, it placed broad-ranging public interaction at the heart of its aims and objectives. It conducted several community programmes to reach out and touch the lives of the most disenfranchised and disempowered in its neighbourhood. It ran a public library, organized summer workshops, a desktop-publishing programme, painting competitions, kite-flying and a slew of events keeping in mind the interests of the Common Man. The Outreach Programme has recently grown to include all activities so far under the purview of the Jamia Cultural Committee. Its task is to give in equal measure to society and to the student body within the university. It therefore makes no distinction between groups and their cultural inheritances. It sees legitimacy in organising, say, a *mushaira* and a folk dance festival, or a play by Shakespeare and one by Habib Tanvir and his troupe of Chhatisgarhi performers. Eclecticism is the key word and weaning the purpose: weaning our students away from narrow definitions of culture and weaning new audiences from far-off places to sample new pleasures.

To come back to the purpose behind this collection of essays, it seemed such a pity that all our efforts over the past few years can be so quickly forgotten A bit like Sisyphus condemned to rolling a boulder up an incline and watching it roll back to the bottom, are we to quietly accept our lot?

April 2009

Rakhshanda Jalil
Jamia Millia Islamia
New Delhi

Contents

Editorial 3

1. The Land of My Dreams: Islamic Liberalism Under Fire In India 13
   Martha C. Nussbaum
2. A Vision For Keeps 29
   Githa Hariharan
3. Terror at Home 33
   Sudhir Chandra
   Translated from Hindi by *Ameena Ansari*
4. Re-living Gandhi's Legacy 37
   Ayesha Siddiqa
5. Presumed Innocent 41
   Mukul Kesavan
6. Living in Jamia Nagar 49
   Rakhshanda Jalil
7. Living A Nightmare with Remarkable Restraint 53
   Rumki Basu
8. Living and Working in Jamia 56
   Lakshmi Subramanian
9. A Community Caught in Myopic Lenses 59
   Meher Fatima Hussain
10. Alienated Generation 65
    Mushirul Hasan
11. Ideas Exchange 68
    Interview with Mushirul Hasan
12. Preserving Our Secular Inheritance 75
    Interview of Mushirul Hasan by Purnima S. Tripathi

Notes on Contributors 79

THE LAND OF MY DREAMS:
Islamic Liberalism Under Fire in India*

MARTHA C. NUSSBAUM

As it became clear that Pakistani Muslims perpetrated the horrendous terrorist attacks in Mumbai last November, many feared a wave of violence against India's own Muslim community. The community, which represents 13.4 percent of Hindu–majority India, suffers from poverty and systemic discrimination, as the government's recent Sachar Commission report documents. It has also been targeted by the Hindu right, which, in 2002, murdered as many as 2,000 people, mostly Muslims, in the state of Gujarat.

That violence, like the violence of Hindu–right mobs against Christians in the eastern state of Orissa in 2008, surely deserves the name of 'terrorism'. Yet, in India as elsewhere, the word 'terrorism' is now frequently confined to the actions of Muslims, and they are suspects almost by virtue of their religion alone. There was reason, then, to fear that mobs would take the Mumbai blasts as the occasion for a renewed assault on an already beleaguered minority.

This assault did not materialize — largely because India's Muslim strongly condemned the terrorist acts and immediately took steps to demonstrate its loyalty to the nation. Muslim cemeteries refused burial to the perpetrators. Muslims wore black armbands on Eid, showing solidarity with mourners of

* *The Boston Review*, March/April 2009.

all religions and nationalities. The world saw a deeply nationalist community, one loyal to the liberal values of a nation that has yet to treat it justly.

It was not the first time India's Muslims have demonstrated a peaceful embrace of the country's founding values. The personal experience of Mushirul Hasan exemplifies the same commitment. A leader of the community, Hasan has been at the center of controversy for his liberal, secular views and has weathered attempts to force him out of his job as Vice-Chancellor of Jamia Millia Islamia, a pluralistic university closely linked to Muslim contributions in India's struggle for nationhood. His story illustrates three aspects of Indian and Muslim life that concerned Western observers regularly ignore.

First, the values we associate with classical liberalism — such as the defense of the freedom of speech, the freedom of conscience, and procedural due process — are not exclusively Western values. During the independence movement in India, they were reinvented by a colonized people who had seen just how little their Western masters honoured such norms.

Second, these values are not tepid and centrist, as we sometimes hear, but rather, truly radical in a world of nations increasingly under pressure both from external violence and from internal quasi-fascist forces.

And finally, Hasan's story shows that there is a distinctive and genuinely Islamic form of liberalism, long–lived and drawing inspiration from religious texts and their central concepts.

Hasan was born on August 15, 1949, exactly two years after the cohort of "midnight's children" whose birth coincided with that of modern India on August 15, 1947. He spent his childhood in cosmopolitan Calcutta (now Kolkata), and later moved North with his family to the Aligarh Muslim University, where his father, a well-known historian, had accepted a post. From early childhood, Hasan encountered the variety and plurality of Muslim life in India.

Then, as now, Muslims were respected as equal citizens by the nation's laws and by some of its citizens, those who followed the lead of Gandhi and Nehru. But Muslims still encountered ubiquitous suspicion and discrimination, and, despite his middle–class upbringing, Hasan was no exception. He once recalled to me how he and his brother were refused when they tried to rent a flat in South Delhi on the grounds that the smell of beef from Muslim kitchens would disgust the local (Hindu) inhabitants.

Hasan received a Ph.D. in history from Cambridge University in 1977 and quickly became one of India's most accomplished and respected historians of the nationalist movement and the modern nation. At the age of thirty–one, he was the youngest historian ever named to a professorial chair in Indi . He took a teaching position at Jamia Millia Islamia and has published a dozen or so well–regarded books on the nationalist struggle, the Nehru family, and the ideas of Gandhi, Nehru, and the liberal Muslims who joined with them.

Hasan addressed the student body, telling them that 'the answer to this is to be more secular, to be more liberal in your outlook, to be more enlightened in your perspective'.

In spite of its name, Jamia has never been a Muslim university. Its location, in a predominantly Muslim residential area, and its historical association with secular liberal Muslims who took leading roles in the independence struggle have made it, over the years, an appealing place for Muslim students, but there has never been preferential admission for Muslims — the admissions form does not even ask the religion of the applicant — and the guiding values of the institution are firmly secular and pluralistic. Today about 60 percent of Jamia Millia Islamia's students and 75 percent of its faculty are Muslim, but inclusiveness is the watchword (as it often is not in Hindu–majority institutions, where both Muslim and lower–caste students routinely suffer stigmatization and harassment).

Rumki Basu, a Hindu woman from West Bengal who currently chairs the university's distinguished Political Science department, explained to me that she never encountered any discrimination or disparagement—even though, right after she got there, she proposed a radical revision of time–honored syllabi, the sort of thing that usually drives at least some colleagues crazy. At Jamia, however, department discussions were always democratic, respectful, and cordial. ('No,' she says, 'I am not making this up.') 'Jamia,' she concludes, 'has busted a lot of unfair stereotypes and myths others hold about Muslims in modern India.' 'Debate, dialogue, and discuss,' these are the principles that define Jamia — and that should be more common at other Indian universities.

In October 1988 Salman Rushdie's *The Satanic Verses* was banned in India. Hasan spoke out publicly against the ban, defending the freedom of speech. A group of radical students in the university, attempting to stop him from teaching, assaulted him physically, inflicting minor injuries. While pressing criminal charges against his assailants, Hasan, who was then Pro Vice-Chancellor of the University, was forced to work from home. He was unable to resume administrative and teaching duties for more than four years. During this time he wrote the excellent book *Legacy of a Divided Nation: India's Muslims Since Independence.*

Eventually he returned to the University, and the values for which he stood — always the institution's dominant values — began to prevail even among its more radical students. Hasan dropped the criminal complaints against the ones who assaulted him (justice moves slowly in India, so by the time Hasan returned to Jamia, they were long since graduates with jobs and families to support), and his mercy made him a popular figure among students of all types. When the Congress Party took over in 2004, the President of the India, following the advice of a three-member selection committee, asked him to become the Vice-Chancellor of the university, equivalent to a U. S. university president.

In September 2008 police investigating a bomb blast in Delhi that had been tentatively linked to Islamic radicalism arrived at the off-campus apartment of some Jamia students. In the ensuing violence, two suspects were killed, one a Jamia student; a police officer later died of his wounds. Two Jamia students were soon arrested on suspicion of aiding terrorism. The students were too poor to pay for competent legal counsel, and, while India's constitution guarantees cost–free legal assistance to 'ensure that opportunities for securing justice are not denied to any citizen by reason of economic or other disabilities,' public defenders are low-grade, and many had recently received threats of violence should they take any case associated with alleged Islamic terrorism. With no hesitation, Hasan said that the university would pay for their legal counsel. The university had done this in other cases, just as it pays students' medical fees. No one objected on those earlier occasions.

But the political charge in the air ensured that this time would be different. The Bharatiya Janata Party (BJP), the political wing of the Hindu right, decided to make an issue of the legal support. Accusing Hasan of misusing public money (Jamia, like all Central Universities in India -, is government-funded), they demanded his resignation. Education Minister Arjun Singh quickly came to Hasan's defense, noting that the money he was using did not come from the government, but from student activity fees and private donations. Like Hasan, he pointed out that the accused are innocent until proven guilty and have a right to a fair trial.

'What do you want us to do?' Hasan asked, 'Stand on a terrace and announce that we are liberal Muslims and that we want to proclaim our loyalty to the nation?'

Meanwhile, Hasan addressed the student body, telling them that 'the answer to this is to be more secular, to be more liberal in your outlook, to be more enlightened in your perspective.' He then led a peace march on the campus, a march so silent, so nonviolent and orderly, that even the press could find no incident of bad behavior to sensationalize. The national media have been decidedly unenthusiastic about Hasan's defense of procedural due process and constitutional norms; they suggest, repeatedly, that he is part of some sinister Muslim cabal. (An honorable exception is *The Hindu*, India's best daily, which published an editorial putting the matter in a balanced perspective; the *Indian Express* and Kolkata's *Telegraph* published valuable op-eds.)

Hasan's fight for basic principles has been won for now, but he still faces a fight in the court of public opinion for the reputation of his university and the honor of its students and teachers. Stereotypes of the violent Muslim are so prevalent in

India — as elsewhere in the world — that it is virtually impossible for Muslim liberals to be taken at their word when they say that they believe in free speech, pluralism, nonviolent persuasion, the rule of law, and the right of each person to a fair trial. 'Oh yes, a screen for darker motives,' is the typical response, pervasive on Hindu blogs and common even in the mainstream press. You say you are a liberal, and that proves you are a radical Islamist.

Meanwhile, hooligans of the Bajrang Dal, a youth movement associated with the Hindu right, have been on a rampage in Orissa, murdering Christians who refuse to reconvert to Hinduism, but the media never refer to this carnage as 'terrorism'. Nor did they use the term 'terrorism' for the Gujarat pogrom. For the media, as for so much of our world, 'terrorism' just means Muslim terrorism. To a skeptical Hindu journalist who had asked him why Muslim intellectuals do not condemn terrorism, Hasan (who had just finished condemning all terrorism, Hindu and Muslim alike) replied:

> You probably don't hear those voices because you don't want to hear those voices. The media doesn't represent those voices because the media is only interested in strident voices. They are not interested in the sane, liberal, rational voices. . . . What do you want us to do? Stand on a terrace and announce that we are liberal Muslims and that we want to proclaim our loyalty to the nation?

Hasan is a remarkable person, but his convictions are hardly *sui generis*. They are deeply rooted in Jamia Millia Islamia's history: a home–grown, tolerant, liberal pluralism has defined the institution from its anti–colonial inception.

The university was born in internal struggles at Aligarh Muslim University, then a conservative institution very much under British control. Many wanted this situation to continue, holding that the mission of Aligarh ought to be to make Indian Muslims 'worthy and useful subjects of the British Crown'. A group of younger intellectuals, however, inspired by Gandhi's ideas and increasingly involved in resistance against the Raj, sought change. Part of their zeal was for Islamic politics: they took a passionate interest in the Khilafat movement, which worked to protect the Ottoman caliphate and sacred Muslim sites from British hijacking. But the Khilafat movement was inherently a campaign against British imperialism, and before long the young radicals of Jamia joined their Turkish concerns to Gandhi's non-cooperation movement, becoming apostles of nonviolent resistance to the local British rulers.

The campus soon split into two camps. The old guard, backed by the British, drove out the young radicals in 1920. Sir George Campbell, the district magistrate, confronted Mohammed Ali, one of the radical leaders, saying, 'You want to bring up these students as disobedient boys.' Ali responded by reciting a verse of the eighteenth-century Urdu poet Mir Taqi Mir that neatly epitomized the behavior of the Raj at this period (though tactfully omitting its heinous acts of violence):

To taunt and sneer and wound and speak unkindly,
She has all these accomplishments, my friend;
Friendship and love and graciousness and kindness
Are things she could never comprehend.

Jamia Millia Islamia was opened the following year. After a short time in Aligarh, it moved to Delhi.

Jamia was born radical. Its curriculum emphasized the study of nationalism as well as the study of Islamic history and the Qu'ran; its admissions policy welcomed male and female, Hindu and Muslim; its pedagogy emphasized debate and contestation in the teaching of all subjects, including religion, denouncing the mere 'passive awareness of dead facts.' The school had strong links with theorists of progressive education such as Bertrand Russell and Rabindranath Tagore and thus gave substantial weight to the arts and vocational education. This philosophy was applied early, since the university included a residential primary school, where 'earning by doing' was the progressive norm. One founder summarized: 'We believe that formal instruction should serve as a support for the exercise of initiative, that the child's mind should be active and responsive, not passive, that the body should be made efficient along with the mind.'

Older students, meanwhile, learned that the national ideal of independence from colonial domination could also become a personal ideal, as Ali stressed:

> Jamia's objective is that Muslims should [not] follow blindly the previous 'fixed' path... the Jamia has instilled hatred in the heart of every student — be he a Muslim or a Hindu — against subjugation by foreign powers. It has kept its air free of transgression and prejudice. For these reasons, the Jamia is both Jamia Millia Islamia and a national university.

The Jamians insisted that identity politics, with its preference for insiders, was foreign to Islam's ideal universal brotherhood.

Jamia was co-educational from the start, but initially the number of female students was small. By 1930, however, the arrival of distinguished female faculty prepared the way for full integration. A later Vice-Chancellor wrote of the way in which the university has helped women 'not only break into the spaces which are male preserves, but also . . . fight back against male tyranny and violence.' Today, women compose about 25 percent of undergraduates, but more than 50 percent of those at the master's degree stage.

Meanwhile, the institution's progressive educational vision led to a stream of visitors from abroad. A distinguished British observer spoke of Jamia as having 'an international breadth of vision' that most Britain-oriented Indian universities lacked. Jamia's degrees were not recognized by the British, but they were recognized in Germany, France, and the United States.

Teachers at Jamia report a glut of detentions and arrests of students. Politicians, the media, and the police try to paint a picture of the university as a hotbed of terrorism.

Jamia's early years were marked by recurrent financial crises. To keep the young institution afloat, a group of distinguished scholars pledged to serve Jamia for twenty years, taking only a token salary. Chief among them was Zakir Hussain, an economist trained in Germany who became Vice-Chancellor in 1928, serving for twenty-one years (and who much later served as the third President of India). A man of tireless energy, enthusiasm, and self–sacrifice, Hussain furthered both the university's educational vision and the nationalist ideal, and did so in close conversation with Gandhi, who viewed Jamia as an important part of a tolerant India. In one letter to the university in 1930, Gandhi wrote:

> Islam enjoins upon us tolerance towards others' religions. It doesn't say that other religions are false. He alone who does good to others is a true man. This is the principle of the [Qu'ran] as also the teaching of other religions. The students of the Jamia, I hope, will spread the message of unity and freedom throughout the country.

The teachers and students of Jamia were passionate about these ideas, as Gandhi acknowledged, saying, 'When I come to the Jamia, I feel I have come home.' Again and again, the faculty wrote about the sort of nationalism they intended to foster: not 'the jingo nationalism of the German or Italian type,' but 'nationalism as a step to internationalism,' 'nationalism of a liberal type.'

After Independence Jamia remained a favorite of the national leadership, Nehru in particular. In a letter of 1952 to Zakir Hussain, Nehru characterized Jamia as a pet project of Gandhi's that he was committed to nurturing. He added a gloomy coda:

> Whatever I can do for Jamia, I shall endeavour to do. The world seems a very dark, dismal and dreary place, full of people with wrong urges or no urge at all, living their lives trivially and without any significance. All the more, therefore, we seek the few sanctuaries and causes and try to derive sustenance from them.

And yet Jamia's financial woes continued. Although some of its degree programs were recognized in 1945, and it achieved nationally recognized university status in 1962, it was only in 1988 that the university was recognized as a Central University, giving it access to more government funds. Having begun as a group of rebels departing from a government-controlled institution (Aligarh), Jamia had finally achieved full recognition by the government of the independent nation.

When Hasan arrived at Jamia, it had a glorious past, but faced many contemporary challenges. Even after it began to receive funds from the central government, it had a hard time becoming the sort of first-rank, cutting-edge university that could compete successfully for students and faculty against Delhi's other prestigious Central Universities, Delhi University and Jawaharlal Nehru University (JNU).

Apart from his massive fundraising efforts, for which he has a gift, Hasan has insistently emphasized the institution's pluralistic, secular character, making it clear to faculty and students from all regions and religions that it can be a very good place to be. One of his successes has been to put Jamia on the map as a dream university for students from some of India's poorest states and regions. Such students might lack the preparation required to get into JNU, but talent and ambition could get them a place in Jamia. Another way Hasan highlights pluralism is by naming buildings after individuals from other nations and religions — including the aforementioned Hindu politician Arjun Singh, who, as Education Minister, has strongly supported the growth of the institution. Meanwhile, empowering faculty such as Basu sends a signal of religious pluralism and sex equality that aids both student and faculty recruitment.

In regard to curriculum, Hasan has strengthened specific areas in which Jamia can compete with the best: thus, a renowned Academy for Third World Studies (founded in 1988, but bolstered under Hasan's leadership); an unparalleled human rights program; and both core and optional courses in public administration, social work, education management, and journalism that are not available in any other university in Delhi. Finally, as Basu emphasizes, Hasan has pushed for an educational climate of tolerance, debate, and difference that few Indian universities, where students raised on rote learning all too often find more of the same, can match.

Hasan's own scholarship has often focused on Jawaharlal Nehru and his accomplishments, so it is not surprising that he sought, for Jamia, the Centre for Jawaharlal Nehru Studies, the first institution of its kind in the country. The Centre opened in October 2004 (shortly after the electoral defeat of the Hindu right and the victory of Congress), with Sonia Gandhi, Congress Party chair, in attendance. In his dedicatory speech, Hasan said that Nehru's legacy is more important in India now than ever because Nehru 'argued for the moral value and legitimacy of nationalism in a form compatible with liberal democratic principles and institutions.' Hasan said that he feels it particularly important to honor Nehru at Jamia, in order to break with the tendency to partition India's heritage by saying to each other, Azad is "yours", Nehru is "ours", Tagore is "ours because we are Bengalis", etc. 'This must stop . . . . We should teach Mir and Ghalib in Bengal, and Tagore and Nazrul Islam in north India .' The Nehru Centre should be a reminder of India's identity as 'tolerant and inclusive', through its invitation to contemplate Nehru's 'own eclectic and broad-minded outlook and the liberal and scientific temper he created in a society that had strong illiberal and authoritarian traits.'

But Hasan also understands, as did Gandhi, that liberal values and nonviolence need to be alluring, not just morally right. Unlike Gandhi, however, Hasan is thoroughly secular, a bon vivant who has a great interest in Urdu poetry and literature. The home he shares with his wife, Zoya, a leading political scientist at JNU and a member of the National Commission for Minorities, is full of beautiful art. And both, as hosts, exemplify Mir's notion of 'graciousness and kindness'. Closer, then, to his hero Nehru, who, despite the bleak tone of many of his letters, was famous for wit and zest at dinner parties.

Hasan, in short, exudes the kind of joyfulness and playfulness that make peple feel that moral principles are not only a duty, but a delight. That is a gift, unfortunately lacking in most of the giants of the Western Enlightenment, though Martin Luther King, Jr., surely had it. Liberal politics is based on respect for the person, but if it does not have something else as well, something more akin to love, it will not capture the hearts of people who long for meaning.

In May a national election may bring to power a coalition government in which the Hindu-nationalist BJP will play a leading role. If that happens, the BJP will no doubt continue their current agenda: attacking moderate Islam, trying to convert what exists at Jamia into the bogeyman of their rhetoric. Only determined public pressure can save the day, ensuring that someone who shares Hasan's commitments, if not he himself (since his term ends this summer), is at the helm during a crucial period of growth and transition for the university.

The story of nonreligious terrorism (for example, the Tamil Tigers) is underreported, and Hindu terrorism against both

Muslims and Christians has yet to appear on the American radar screen.

Other needs are even more pressing in the short term. The National Human Rights Commission has notified the Delhi police that it is investigating the bloody September 2008 incident and wants a complete report. The police write-up is, indeed, full of inconsistencies and gaps. For example, the police arrived at the student dwelling without backup and without bulletproof vests, as if they were not preparing to encounter armed terrorists — yet, in retrospect, they say this is exactly what they were doing. The dwelling where the policeman was shot had only one entrance, yet we are supposed to believe that, with police lined up at the door, two students managed to escape unharmed. The students in the house had submitted the usual residential questionnaire with correct names, dates of birth, etc., all rather odd if their student identities were a ruse and they were really members of a widespread Muslim terrorist organization (the Indian Mujahideen), as is alleged. Finally, the two students whose legal fees Jamia is paying have a clean record, and all who know them describe them as peaceful, even dreamy and impractical. So we urgently need to know the quality of the evidence linking them to the case.

Meanwhile, teachers at Jamia report a glut of detentions and arrests of students. Politicians, the media, and the police try to paint a picture of the university as a hotbed of terrorism, and large numbers of students in off-campus housing have been asked to vacate their flats by landlords who fear police reprisals. Police presence all around the campus is distressing, disrupting the climate of instruction. The unfairness of disturbing an entire university of 14,000 students over the alleged actions of two of its members is obvious, but hardly anyone is complaining about it, apart from the teachers and students themselves.

Perhaps the most alarming aspect of the Jamia case is the atmosphere surrounding those who provide legal counsel to people accused of terrorism. One after another, bar associations in different parts of the country are announcing boycotts of terror suspects. In Madhya Pradesh, two suspects were forced to hire counsel from a different state after all local lawyers refused them. A leading state BJP official supported the boycott, saying that 'a distinction must be made between criminals and terrorists' So much for the presumption of innocence. In Uttar Pradesh, lawyers have been faced with threats to their safety if they take on terror cases. Legal and social activists believe that the Hindu right has profoundly infiltrated the mechanisms of criminal justice making it very difficult for Muslims to get a fair trial. Often, moreover, Muslims remain in detention without trial for years. Muslims constitute 18 percent of convicts in Indian prisons, 21.8 percent of those whose cases are currently being tried, and 37.2 percent of those in detention awaiting either trial or specific charges.

When the legal system works this badly, essential constitutional rights become mere words on paper. Moreover, the rhetoric of the Hindu right, which constantly equates arrest with conviction, suggests at best a tenuous commitment to the rule of law. The contention that offering legal aid means being 'soft on terrorism' — a ubiquitous charge against Hasan, despite his repeated condemnations of terrorism in any form — is a communitarian idea that betrays impatience with the very idea of due process. When lots of people in a democracy think this way, there is danger. In India its source has been the same for decades: a Hindu right that never accepted the liberal values of equal respect, due process, and religious non-establishment.

Hasan's ordeal leaves us with four conclusions.

First, we should mistrust stereotypes of the violent Muslim. Current preconceptions, combined with media sensationalism, lead to selective reporting (in India as elsewhere). Stories of Muslim liberals provoke boredom or skepticism. But the failure to report only confirms the preconceptions. Meanwhile, the story of nonreligious terrorism (for example, the Tamil Tigers) is underreported, and Hindu terrorism against both Muslims and Christians has yet to appear on the American radar screen. As Hasan points out, we need more prominent stories of Muslim nonviolence:

> A whole auditorium can be filled up with books on Islam and violence but what about Islam and nonviolence? What about Gaffar Khan [a Muslim associate of Gandhi's, who developed a

> philosophy of nonviolence using Islamic sources]? Does he not exist or is he of no consequence because he does not fit the stereotype that some people wish to create and perpetuate about an entire community?

For this reason, one of Hasan's current priorities is the creation on Jamia's campus of a museum of the nationalist struggle, devoted to the history elided at other museums: the prominent role played by Muslims in the nationalist movement. While we wait for the museum to be built, the book *Partners in Freedom*, which Hasan co-authored with Rakhshanda Jalil, tells the story in both text and photographs.

Second, the stereotyping of Muslims as violent, when combined with economic and political discrimination, engenders among Muslims a justified anger that can all too easily spill over into unjustified violence. Gandhi knew well that the rage of his followers against the British had legitimate roots, yet he was able to convince people that the best response to oppression was nonviolent protest.

Mushirul Hasan follows Gandhi's program. In fact, I am tempted to say, somewhat hyperbolically, that virtually the only place in today's India where Gandhi's ideas are being duly honored is on the campus of Jamia. But Hasan knows, like Gandhi, and like Martin Luther King, Jr., that anger will not go away, will not cease to create the possibility of violence unless the subordination that fuels it is brought to an end.

Therefore, while working to promote nonviolence, one must also work to eradicate political and economic conditions that nourish the desire for violence. Noting the economic discrimination suffered by India's Muslims (the lack of basic social services, such as clean water, in the poor residential areas surrounding Jamia is one ugly example) — now compounded by widespread political discrimination in the form of round–ups on suspicion of terrorism (India's analogue to the odious American tradition of racial profiling) and, more worrying, threats against lawyers who defend people accused of terrorism — Hasan says to that same skeptical reporter: 'The fact that they are still liberals in this sort of situation — caught between the devil and the deep sea — you should give them a Padma award.'(The Padma Shri award is given by the Indian government each year to people who have performed some meritorious service to the nation. Hasan was awarded the Padma Shri in 2007.)

The third conclusion to be drawn from these events is the Gandhian one: the importance of the nonviolent response. Speaking about Muslim communities more generally, Hasan insists that the solution to Muslims' problems lies in nonviolence and a grass-roots demand for democracy:

> The stranglehold of the orthodoxy, especially in its political and religious form, has to be loosened and slackened. The answer lies in more and more Muslim communities moving towards democracy. There is no short cut to democracy. . . . There is no place for pharaohs in the modern world.

Hasan thus joins such anti-theocratic Muslims as Akbar Ganji of Iran in calling for a restructuring of Islamic nations through a popular demand for democratic self-government, prominently including a commitment to the equality and empowerment of women. And he immediately adds that the move to democracy has been very much impeded by attempts on the part of the United States to impose democracy by force.

The final, and perhaps most important, lesson is that, following Gandhi, we must all rethink our understandings of strength and weakness, courage and timidity. Real strength, in an individual, is not manifested by bashing people over the head. Who does that? Only someone who feels threatened and weak. Real strength is manifested by the ability to show respect to others, to treat them as equals, and not to try to impose one's will by force. Real strength in a community or a nation, similarly, is manifested not by a willingness to dispose of liberal values whenever violence seems easier or more fun, but by a commitment to them that does not bend when the going gets tough. That is radical. And if being radical means going 'to the root' of the matter, it is the liberal, who subdues the violence and greed of the self, who is the true radical, while left and right communitarians casually allow the banal and constant desire for domination to carry the day.

In a world where so many anthems call for blood and equate

manliness with abuse, here is what Jamia's founders wrote for its students to sing as the official anthem of the university:

> *Here conscience alone is the beacon . . .*
> *It's the Mecca of many faiths,*
> *Traveling is the credo here, pausing a sacrilege. . .*
> *Cleaving against currents is the creed here,*
> *The pleasure of arrival lies in countering crosscurrents.*
> *This is the home of my yearnings,*
> *This is the land of my dreams.*

A radical song indeed.

A VISION FOR KEEPS*

GITHA HARIHARAN

It's that time of the year again, when conditioned by custom, we conjure up images of the year that was. The point of such an exercise is to be enriched in some way. I for one like looking back on the year and its events so that I can choose something — a few words, maybe an image or two — to take with me across the border to the new year.

This year the exercise seemed a difficult one to begin with. What happened in Mumbai appeared to have diminished the rest of the year and made it irrelevant. I knew this was neither true nor rational, but that's how it felt for a while. The shock of the Mumbai attacks settled into sadness, deepened by the war-speaking cacophony pushing its way centre stage in the place of mature reaction.

Then luckily I was invited to see a building in Delhi that was almost done. This modern building with its clean lines and elegant façade is going to be home to a large number of books and, hopefully, a large number of readers — generations of them. I walked around the spacious and empty halls of what will be the new library in Jamia Millia Islamia. There is one hall that especially invited me to linger there. This is a spacious hall, bordered on one side by a marvellous arc-shaped corridor. On the other side, it has large windows that frame the sunlit sky and trees outside. I found myself liking the hall even better

* *The Telegraph*, Sunday 28 December 2008.

when I was told that this is the general reading room. Not only will it be open to the undergraduates, but also, on certain days, to the community. The people in the locality are going to have some share in this library.

On this site still in the process of becoming, the evidence of construction all around me, I may have found the image of hope I was looking for. The fact that this new library is at the Jamia, and that it's called the Dr Zakir Husain Library is part of the message of hope.

To me the library is a fresh reminder of Jamia's rich inheritance. And this is an inheritance worth recalling because it suits some to invent their own communalized version of Jamia in the wake of events such as the Batla House encounter.

What is this "rich inheritance"? I have spent some time on the campus as writer-in-residence, and I have learnt a little about the vision that led its founders to set up Jamia. I have also learnt something of the complicated ways in which national events and processes influenced the evolution of the Jamia idea and institution.

The story of Jamia and its inheritance began in Aligarh. The Jamia idea was born in the throes of anti-colonial activism. The Khilafat movement fed into this activism; so did the larger aspiration for independence, which was articulated through the non-cooperation movement. The Jamia was set up in 1921 and its basic objective was to balance religious and national identities. An article in *Hamdard* in 1926 stated that "Jamia's objective is that Muslims should neither follow blindly the previous 'fixed' path, nor should they believe that the essence of religion lies in a few problems of jurisprudence... the Jamia has instilled hatred in the heart of every student — be he a Muslim or a Hindu — against subjugation by foreign powers. It has kept its air free of transgression and prejudice. For these reasons, the Jamia is both Jamia Islamia and a national university."

Jamia means university, and Millia refers to its national character. The founders were supported by Gandhi, who insisted the name should remain Jamia Millia Islamia and not be changed to National Muslim University. Together they built up Jamia "stone by stone", said Sarojini Naidu, and "sacrifice by sacrifice". Men such as Hakim Ajmal Khan hoped to make Hindu children learn something of Islam and Muslim children learn something of Hinduism. They hoped a "united Indian nationalism" would emerge from this knowledge each community would gain of the other, a nationalism that was meant to be both pragmatic and non-sectarian.

Perhaps a description of a *Qaumi Hafta* (community week) organized in 1927 to commemorate the massacre at Jallianwala Bagh explains what some of these ideas meant in practice. For a week, the housekeeping staff were given leave and the boys and faculty did all the work. Such Gandhian projects sometimes called for sweeping the streets in Karol Bagh — where the university then had its modest temporary "campus". Or the boys went door-to-door, distributing spinning wheels and cotton, taking back the spun cotton and weaving it into *khadi*, or arranging public awareness programmes on health and hygiene among the poor in the neighbourhood. The mayhem that followed Partition did affect Jamia — how could it not? But its campus remained peaceful; Gandhi described it, at that point, as "an oasis of peace in the Sahara".

To get back to the present, and to the new library. For a university traditionally starved of funds — to the extent that the faculty had to accept cuts in their salaries for many years — it is poetic justice that it finally has a big new library. The library is also named exactly as it should be. It is named for Zakir Husain, who devoted so many years of his life to building Jamia, to keeping it alive, and to nurturing it with his democratic style of functioning. For Zakir Husain, Jamia had a distinct task and vision. The task was to prepare "a roadmap for the future lives of Indian Muslims with the religion of Islam at its core", but this map was to be filled with the multifarious colours of "the civilization of India", and, in particular, "the life of the common man". The basis of the vision was the belief that true education of their religion would imbibe in Indian Muslims "a love for their country and a passion for national integration... and prepare them to take active part in seeking independence and progress for India..."

In the long history of any institution there are, of course, ups and downs, periods when the founders' vision shines with meaning, and other more stagnant times. But it is important — for all those associated with Jamia, for those who are afraid of what they think it stands for, and for those who vilify it, to remember its origins. Jamia was conceived as an entity with a liberal orientation, and this orientation continues to be part of its world view. Hopefully the new library and its contents will help reassert the secular vision which is an intrinsic part of Jamia's identity, the belief that the "brotherhood of man" was the only "real tie". An image of hope for the near future: in the place of fear and suspicion, may there be, in the rooms of this new library, in the words of the educationist, K.G. Saiyidain, "the joy of intellectual quest, a sense of championship with many kindred minds and spirits which transcended differences of language, caste and creed, a love of books and a passport into the world of ideas...."

TERROR AT HOME*

SUDHIR CHANDRA
Translated from Hindi by Ameena Ansari

'Home' and 'outside' have no fixed meanings. They vary contextually. Like the self and the other. There are, nonetheless, occasions in life when some relationships are formed, never to change.

It has been thirty years since I left Jamia Millia Islamia. I'd gone there in 1965. 'Gone there' doesn't sound quite right. Showing great affection, like he were entreating me, Professor Mujeeb, the Vice-Chancellor, had asked me to join. I left Jamia in 1977. To tell the truth, I was compelled to leave.

In a way it was good. With the severance of this association, it became almost a habit to break free from other bonds. I began enjoying nomadising.

However, neither nomadising nor the bitter severance of my association with Jamia dented the relationship I had formed with the institution during Mujeeb Sahib's time. No matter how rarely I have visited Jamia during the last thirty years, that intimate bond has remained unaffected. I cannot remain indifferent to the ups and downs of Jamia.

What has really got me thinking is the way this month's bomb explosions by terrorists have got linked not only to Jamia Nagar but also to Jamia Millia. And, if I may say so, despite the fear of being called obsessive, I have been thinking a bit too much about it all. Why have I started thinking so obsessively

* *Jansatta*, September 2008.

about the kind of terrorism being linked to Muslims, especially Muslim youth?

My thirteen years at Jamia Millia Islamia, and subsequently two and a half years at Aligarh Muslim University, have taught me ways of perception which the best books of history, sociology and psychology never can. As a Hindu, living in my own country, I have come to understand the psyche of the minority community. One who suffers not, knows not the suffering of others. To understand what goes on, or does not go on, in the hearts and minds of the minority community, the majority has to inculcate sensitivity and be extremely perceptive. Only then can there be any meaningful discussion on what minority minds think, or do not think. And something done to rectify the situation.

I am well aware that my own social scientist friends will excoriate me for bringing up the issue of Muslim psyche. They will remind me that Muslims from different regions and classes are not one, that there are innumerable internal differentiations amongst them. The hearts and minds of which Muslims, then, am I invoking? I am talking of every Muslim – of almost every Muslim, if I am forced to weigh my words – of the country. This is so because the country's majority community has compelled Muslims to feel like one community. Whether one wishes it or not, everyone bearing a Muslim name is, just for bearing that name, forced to think of themselves as Muslims. A Muslim in the country today will have to be very self-centred and insensitive to disavow her/his Muslim identity.

Their willed or forced identity as Muslims, the helplessness of being isolated and viewed with suspicion, the pain and humiliation of being so treated, the resultant terror which can any moment turn real, and every time it turns real it is more terrorising than the last time, there is nothing in their own country that can save the Muslims from this dismal reality. No matter how prominent, how influential, or how distinguished, a Muslim can be insulted and persecuted anytime, anywhere.

This shared wretchedness does not mean, however, that all the Muslims in the country think, or can think, alike. That they have no faith in lawful and constitutional methods. That all of them support violence and terrorism.

Which is what many Hindus have started believing. And, unfortunately, the number of such Hindus is rapidly increasing.

I do not know what I can do, or how I can say things, in order that such Hindus, shedding their preconceived notions for a moment, may think about the Muslims with some restraint. I do try to have on this matter a discussion that is calm, logical and cordial. But often—both with family and friends—tensions glide into the atmosphere even before we get talking. A cousin of mine — he is also a dear friend — at the mere mention of Muslims bursts out against me, 'So, Maulana ...'

When I was teaching at the Aligarh Muslim University, a Hindu friend asked me, 'How many Hindus teach there besides you?' The question was not inspired by curiosity. The man already knew everything. Without saying anything, he was through his hostile question exposing the supposed narrow-mindedness and communalism of the Muslims. I answered, 'Of course I'll tell you that, and I'll also tell you the number of Hindu students at the Aligarh Muslim University. But you must first tell me if you have ever tried to find out the ratio of Hindu-Muslim teachers and students at the Banaras Hindu University.'

As I write this, I am reminded of a similar episode from my student days. I was then living in Allahabad University's Sir Sunder Lal Hostel. It was the season for new admissions. One day some hostellers created a furore because a Muslim had been admitted to our hostel. Dr. B. B. Saxena, the Hostel Superintendent, immediately called a meeting and enquired why the admission of a Muslim was being objected to. He was asked, in great agitation, why a Muslim had been admitted to Sir Sunder Lal Hostel when the University had provided a separate hostel for Muslim students. Dr. Saxena riposted, 'This University also has a separate hostel for Hindus. Why don't you all go there?'

Both examples reflect a particular kind of mentality. Certain things happen, without being visible, under the influence of that mentality.

It is not that the person placing the Aligarh Muslim University in the dock was unaware of the Hindu University. Nor were those opposing the admission of a Muslim to Sir Sunder Lal Hostel ignorant of the existence of a separate hostel for Hindu students. But under the influence of that mentality, both these facts appeared completely differently. The Hindus, as per that mentality, constitute the 'we', that is, the country. Whatever is the country's is 'ours'. Where 'we', the Hindus, are, there everyone is. Where we are not, there is the need to ask questions, to be vigilant, and to reform.

Gripping the Hindus rapidly, this mentality is to some extent natural. It has its historical, psychological and other reasons. This, too, must be understood. What is imperative, though, is the need for this mentality to understand itself and, following that understanding, change itself. Should it fail to see through its naturalness, it will destroy that – the country – which it equates with the Hindus.

Since 1990, I have seen innocent young Muslims being drawn towards terrorism. The first time it was in Vyara, a south Gujarat town where, vainly trying to curb his anger against the pitiless violence of Hindutva, a Muslim motor mechanic said, 'We, too, can become terrorists.' And in 1993, following the post-6 December 1992 Hindutva barbarity on Muslims in Bombay and Surat, terrorism did, indeed, explode one day. Those who have witnessed Gujarat 2002, with its Shah Alam-like camps and its Naroda-Patiya-like perversion, would recall the faces that struggled to keep their impotent fury inside. How much did those faces want to speak, and how much they struggled to suppress all that, lest the fury be frittered away in words!

One can't say how honestly the state machinery and its penal system will do what they must. But the society — especially the right thinking ones among the majority community — must realise that exterminating terrorists will not exterminate terrorism.

I have witnessed terror in my own home. The first time in 1984 in Delhi. Then in 1992 in Surat. It was in Surat that a helpless Muslim woman, pointing to a girl standing mutely beside her, had shouted in a hoarse broken voice, 'Bhai, they did *that* to this girl!' Then it happened in 2002 in Baroda and Ahmedabad. Now I have seen terror in reverse in Delhi. It has got linked with Jamia. With those who could have been my own students—my very own children.

If 'we' fail to see our own 'terrorising', we shall fail to stop what we call 'terrorism'.

RE-LIVING GANDHI'S LEGACY*

AYESHA SIDDIQA

In this day and age when one desperately searches for men of vision, courage and integrity it is such a relief to know of a man like Prof Mushirul Hasan, the vice chancellor of New Delhi's Jamia Millia Islamia.

An established historian, he will be remembered by posterity for his liberal views, enlightened thought and efforts to heal the wounds of a community that has a significant presence in Indian society. This is in reference to the mother-father role that Mushirul Hasan played in calming down the Muslim community in Jamia Nagar and the Muslim students of Jamia Millia who were extremely fearful after some students were picked up by the Delhi police in connection with the seven blasts in the Indian capital.

The vice chancellor established a fund to which teachers and old students of the university contributed to provide legal aid to the ten arrested Jamia students.** Of course this brought lots of criticism from many in India. They were of the view that the university or its office-holders had no business to help the students because then every student anywhere in the country could seek similar assistance.

Mushir's act became even more noticeable after the vice chancellors of universities in Gujarat decided that all students

---

* *The Dawn, Karachi,* 17 October 2008.

** Of the ten arrested suspects, two are Jamia students. —Editor of all colleges and universities in the state must take a course in anti-terrorism. Furthermore, the Gujarat VCs declared that in the event of the police arresting someone under suspicion of terrorism, the detainee in question would be considered a terrorist. This stance is diametrically opposed to Mushir's position.

One hopes that those who fault the Jamia's VC for helping his students will realise that his act will strengthen rather than weaken the Indian state and society. It is an important symbolic gesture in a society where communities today are becoming increasingly estranged. While the developments post-9/11 have changed global politics, they have also created bitterness between the majority and a sizeable minority in India. The liberal and seemingly secular elite in India view Muslims with a lot of suspicion and this in turn draws a reaction from the minority community.

Some would argue that suspicion is natural in the current circumstances. However, there are always two sides to a story. The other side, which the majority might not wish to see, is that given the increased hostility towards religious minorities in India, namely Muslims and Christians, the minority communities are bound to feel ostracised and bitter about the state. The Muslims in Kashmir are one part of the story, but the other reality pertains to the rest of India where Muslims feel less secure especially after the Babri Masjid incident and the Gujarat carnage.

These two incidents widened the chasm which, in any case, existed due to the disparity in development. The majority of Muslims are less educated and poor. They are not even impressed by the few examples of success found in Bollywood in the shape of Shahrukh Khan, Aamir Khan or Salman Khan. Or some of the cricket stars.

Some might argue this is the fault of the Muslim leadership in India that has done little to develop the community. But then isn't it the responsibility of the state as well to assist the poor people of a community which once had a proud sense of ownership in the Indian state? Or isn't it the responsibility of the state to bring development to the poorer segments irrespective of the community they belong to?

What we see as violence in India is a repercussion of imbalanced development. The country may be a regional power with nuclear weapons and blue-water capability but it is also a place where a large segment of the population does not get a share in the development windfall. On the one hand is the growing middle class, which has access to education and resources. This is the emerging class which, like in any other part of the world, suffers from myopia and would like to shut its eyes to poverty and the dispossessed.

In their view, Muslims represent a bunch of terrorists. It is sad that India, which claims to be the epitome of secularism, has also become a society where the growing middle class is increasingly prone to stereotyping the other community. So when discussions take place in most affluent living rooms, Muslims are dismissed as a bunch of troublemakers and a violent lot.

The question for such people is, what does India plan to do with the Muslims who account for 14-15 per cent of the total population? Does it plan to drown them in the Indian Ocean or force them to carve out yet another country for themselves? And let's not forget the Christians who are being targeted as well. After all, these people chose to remain Indians in 1947 and are the country's citizens.

Recently, during a chat with a senior university professor from Jawaharlal Nehru University, my suggestion that India is under threat from within was brushed aside with the argument that the country is too large and can absorb crises. The problem is that no country is large enough when the crisis it faces is the intolerance of the majority. Furthermore, the concern in the region is that if anything happens to India due to internal security issues, its large size will negatively impact the entire region.

The idea is not that the country will disintegrate. After all there are other battles being fought in India as well. There are the Naxalites, the Assamese and Kashmiris who are fighting their own battles. However, communal tension is far more lethal especially in this day and age when people believe that violence may be their weapon of last resort. A divided society cannot be set right even with an armoury of lethal weapons. Perhaps what university students in Gujarat need is a lesson in tolerance rather than counter-terrorism.

Therefore, what Mushir has done is show courage and vision to protect the Indian state. Many have tried to remind him that the Jamia is the very place he was kicked out of for not supporting the anti-Rushdie fatwa and resultant demonstrations. So then why support such people? It is probably his faith in the Indian state that made him take a stand. Unfortunately, many would rather communalise his decision rather than support it. One wishes that there were VCs, professors and intellectuals from the majority community who would come together to heal the wounds of the various minorities in the country.

At the end of the day, Mushirul Hasan represents Gandhi's legacy better than many others. One sincerely hopes that India finds more men of vision and similar character to save itself from violence and internal battles.

PRESUMED INNOCENT

MUKUL KESAVAN

I teach in Jamia Millia Islamia, a university in Delhi that was in the news because two young men said to be terrorists were killed in its vicinity on 19 September, 2008, in the course of an 'encounter' or shoot out with the police. One of these men was a student of the university. Subsequently the police made more arrests in connection with the recent bomb blasts in Delhi and two of those arrested were enrolled in Jamia.

The university authorities made it clear that they would deal strictly with any student found to be involved in terrorism. The university also declared that it would provide legal aid to the arrested students (a) because they were members of Jamia in good standing; and (b) till such time as their guilt was proved they were entitled to due process.

The response to this declaration was at once odd and unsurprising. Various spokespersons for the BJP demanded that the Vice-Chancellor be sacked for using the public purse (Jamia is a UGC-funded Central University) for succouring terrorists. The Vice-Chancellor of a university in Jodhpur, in the course of a speech inaugurating a seminar on 'Indian Women: Changes and Challenges', found the time to regret that Jamia's 'kulapati' was supporting terrorists.

These reactions aren't just odd, they're contrary to every intuition Indians have about their republic and about civil society. We're a constitutional republic, a nation of laws. Mr Ravi Shankar Prasad, the spokesman of the BJP, almost certainly knows that Article 39 A of our Constitution sets out the principle of legal aid. It does so because the presumption of innocence and the right to a free trial become meaningful only if the accused has proper legal representation. Once we allow that public money can, indeed must be spent to ensure that people have legal representation, it becomes hard to find a charitable explanation for the BJP's outrage.

I have a son who, in less than two years, will go to university. If, god forbid, he finds himself in police remand for whatever reason (murder, armed robbery, menacing the faculty, fraud), I'd want his university to behave as if it were acting in my place, in loco parentis. I would expect the Proctor of the university to liaise with the Station House Officer to make sure that such rights of visitation as he might have in that ghastly circumstance were given him, to hire a lawyer to see if he could be released on bail, and if the nature of the alleged offence didn't allow that, to try to have him transferred to judicial custody. Police remand is a dreadful form of imprisonment in India; unlike judicial custody where the procedural restraints of prison manuals apply, the police in their station house lockups have a free hand in working suspects over. Any university which washes its hands off its students the moment they are arrested by the police because it doesn't want to be associated with notoriety or (as in this case) the taint of terrorism, is a cringing and wretched institution undeserving of a citizen's respect or a parent's trust.

Interestingly, Jamia has supplied legal aid to arrested students before. Some years ago, dozens of its students were arrested on charges that were later shown to be unfounded. But their innocence isn't relevant: the point is that no one thought at that time to object to the university's aid. The reason for the difference isn't hard to find. The previous incident involved a skirmish on the campus; this time round the students were suspected of collusion in terror. But it wasn't just the gravity of the offence that made the difference; the narrative that the BJP hoped to exploit was that of jihadi terrorism and the two useful facts they were rubbing together like flints were i) that these students were Muslims and ii) that Jamia Millia

Islamia is a remarkably Muslim sounding name. 'Muslim university bats for Muslim terrorists': for a party whose reason for being is the demonization of minorities, specifically Muslims, this was a script made in heaven.

So some background is in order. Jamia Millia Islamia began life as a nationalist college. It was born of the Non-Cooperation movement, the first anti-colonial mass agitation led by Mahatma Gandhi. A group of young radical students and alumni of the Aligarh Muslim University, dissatisfied with their alma mater's compradore politics, decided to establish a nationalist, anti-colonial alternative to AMU. Gandhi, Maulana Mohammad Ali, Dr Zakir Hussain, Hakim Ajmal Khan, Dr. M.A. Ansari are only some of the great names who nurtured Jamia. It's not just ironical, it's grotesque that the BJP, born of parent organizations like the RSS and the Hindu Mahasabha that were notable for their distance from the great anti-colonial struggles that won India freedom, should make a bid to impugn Jamia's commitment to India's integrity.

But history aside, it's worth reflecting on the way in which we respond to news related to terrorist atrocity. In the Jamia encounter, a policeman and two terror suspects were killed. Years of staged shootouts have induced a reflexive scepticism about police encounters. In this case a policeman was killed which seemed to suggest that someone was shooting back. However given the police's fraught relations with Muslim neighbourhoods, this fact cut very little ice with residents of Jamia Nagar. But even if we allow that on the face of it the police had reason to raid the premises in which these two young men were killed, the complete lack of concern in the majority of news reports that two young men had been summarily killed (Atif was in his early twenties and Sajid was all of seventeen) was dismaying.

In the summer of 2005 the British police killed Jean Charles de Menezes, a Brazilian with a brown skin because they were convinced he was a terrorist. He wasn't; it was a dreadful mistake and though it was made in good faith, three years later, the inquest into the incident now threatens the career of Britain's top policeman, Ian Blair. It's at least possible that the Delhi

Police, likewise, got it wrong, that Atif or Sajid or both were innocent, that they were caught in the wrong place at the wrong time but nearly every newspaper I read baldly reported the death of two terrorists without any caveats or qualifications.

The synchronised bombings that have ravaged Indian cities over the past year have led the police, unsurprisingly, to look for Muslim villains. It has led political commentators from the Hindutva right to make interesting distinctions. One worthy tried to distinguish Muslim terrorists from Hindu rioters and pogrom artists. A rioter, he argued, could, a few years after the riot, settle down into society again as a solid citizen. A terrorist, on the other hand, was implacably committed to the subversion of the state. I can see what he means: Gujarat is full of solid citizens who looted and killed recreationally a few years ago and now lead respectable lives unmolested by the police.

But given the fact that the most recent explosions in Modasa (Gujarat) and Malegaon (Mahrashtra) occurred in Muslim localities and had mainly Muslims casualties, the police might try to diversify their enquiries. It was only two years ago that two members of a Hindu militia blew themselves up in Nanded while making a powerful bomb. When people, policemen and political parties buy into the narrative of an exclusive and a priori Muslim guilt, they run the risk of turning this remarkable republic into an ordinary, ugly, majoritarian state.

* * *

In November 2008, less than two months after the Batla House encounter near Jamia Millia Islamia, the investigative agencies in Maharashtra took a *sadhvi*, Pragnya Singh and a serving army officer, Colonel Purohit, into custody for their alleged involvement in the terrorist explosions at Malegaon. After the BJP's denunciation of the university authorities at Jamia Millia Islamia for their decision to extend legal aid to two students arrested for suspected involvement in terrorist conspiracy, it was good to see the party belatedly embrace that civilized republican principle, the presumption of innocence.

The arrest of Sadhvi Pragnya Singh and Lt Col. Purohit, , spurred the party (after some initial hesitation) to affirm their innocence and to offer the Sadhvi the best legal representation available in the country. The Anti-Terrorist Squad (ATS) and its investigations of Pragnya Singh and Col Purohit for terrorist activity were condemned by the spokespersons of the Sangh Parivar as politically motivated and unsound.

None of this criticism was unreasonable. The accused were entitled to a fair trial and good lawyers are an indispensable part of due process; moreover, the tendency of the Indian police and its investigative agencies to feed newspapers and news channels with unreliable information and spurious breakthroughs in cases that are never resolved, leads to an understandable skepticism about their claims. The BJP was also right in taking exception to the term 'Hindu terrorism' used by lazy journalists; even if Colonel Purohit and Sadhvi Pragnya Singh were to be found guilty, no connection between being Hindu and being terrorist would follow from their guilt. In the event of their conviction, the proper term for their activities would be 'Hindutvavadi terror': to assimilate a large and law-abiding community to the violence of bigots would be unjust.

The BJP was also right in arguing that members of India's armed forces should not be carelessly implicated by police agencies in something as serious as terrorism. Not because soldiers should be seen to be above the law or be privileged by it, but because the political neutrality of the army is a precious asset and charging an officer with political extremism is a serious business, not to be lightly undertaken. The Indian army is a curious institution, built on pluralist ideas that are colonial rather than republican in their provenance, but in times of sectarian violence it is often summoned to establish order becauseunlike the police, it is seen as a secular, apolitical force. So if the BJP's affirmation of Colonel Purohit's innocence helped to ensure a thorough investigation and a fair trial, the party would have done all Indians a favour.

Equally, Mr Advani's condemnation of the 'narco' tests administered to the Sadhvi (and Lt Col Purohit) was consistent with the long held position of human rights activists that forcing suspects to endure potentially dangerous chemical injections to induce legally worthless confessions is both barbaric and illegal. 'Brain mapping' and 'narco testing' are good examples of the ways in which Indian policemen use pseudo-scientific gimcrackery as a substitute for real police work.

So on these issues every Indian who believes in the rule of law should endorse the BJP's criticism of the Anti-Terrorism Squad. The Sadhvi's allegations that she was beaten and tortured in police custody should have been taken seriously. Mr Advani's demand that the Sadhvi and Lt Col Purohit be investigated by a judicial probe and not the ATS ought to have been given fair consideration. The fact that the BJP and its allies were pleased with the rough 'justice' meted out to the two men shot by the police in the Batla House 'encounter' and subsequently wanted Jamia's arrested students left indefinitely in police custody, unaided by the university to which they were affiliated, doesn't in itself invalidate the importance of human rights and due process.

The real difficulty with the Sangh Parivar's defence of Sadhvi Pragnya Singh and Lt Col Purohit lies in the reasons its spokespersons adduce for their innocence. Dr. Praveen Togadia, the chief of the Vishwa Hindu Parishad, made the Hindutva-vadi case without qualifications: "No Hindu can be a terrorist" he declared. Asked if he knew the sadhvi, he said: "I do not know Pragnya Singh at all. But I know she is not a terrorist." For Dr. Togadia, Ms Singh's birth identity was all the evidence he needed to know that the allegations against her were false. He said as much: "Hindus will not forget this. They [the police and the Congress] are committing the sin of describing a Hindu, a 'sadhvi', as a terrorist ... I warn that there will be a political backlash and the government will be swept out." (*The Hindu*)

Chandan Mitra, MP and the Editor of *The Pioneer*, made the same point more circumspectly. "Let the courts pronounce the "Hindu terrorists" guilty" he wrote in the *Economic Times*, "and, if so, let the verdicts be executed. But they cannot be pilloried on the basis of specious "confessions", which could well be figments of a beleaguered ATS's shaky imagination." Aware that this might seem inconsistent with the Sangh Parivar's enthusiasm for pillorying Muslims accused of terrorist conspiracy by Anti-Terrorist Squads elsewhere (such as the students arrested after the Batla House encounter near Jamia Millia Islamia), Mitra argued that Muslims accused of terrorism were a different matter. Muslims had form in the matter of terrorist conspiracy whereas Hindus didn't.

"Many SIMI and other jihadi terror mongers have already been brought to book and being tried in courts. The most celebrated of the lot, Afzal Guru, has been found guilty by the Supreme Court and sentenced to death." It's worth remembering that one SIMI member, Yasin Patel, has been successfully prosecuted under a terrorism law. Three others were recently jailed for a year, not for terrorism but for stoking communal hatred. Even if there was to be a string of successful terror prosecutions against SIMI, are we to understand that Mitra would have the police and the public withhold the presumption of innocence from Muslims in cases of terrorist conspiracy?

This is rather like arguing that once Hindus are convicted of terrorizing and murdering Muslims during the Gujarat pogroms, or slaughtering Sikhs in the Delhi pogrom of 1984, any Hindu accused of communal killing afterwards can be legitimately treated as guilty unless proven innocent, whereas Muslims and Sikhs charged with communal violence ought to continue to be given the benefit of the doubt.

In essence, there is no difference in Chandan Mitra's position and Dr Togadia's. They both believe that Hindu violence can't be described as terror because Hindus are victims. Victims can't be perpetrators. So even if the ATS case against Pragnya Singh and Srikant Purohit is successfully prosecuted, even if they are guilty of organizing the explosions in Malegaon, they aren't terrorists because all they're doing is retaliating against jihadi violence:

"Even if for a moment we accept that some Hindus have indulged in copycat acts", writes Chandan Mitra, "it must be borne in mind that the majority of Indians are shocked, outraged, angry and even vengeful because of relentless terrorist depredations. Nearly 10,000 innocent people have died at the hands of bloodthirsty jihadi terrorists over the past 15 years. If some people, howsoever misguided, attempt to avenge this because the state fails to provide security or succour should it come as a big surprise? This is not to justify vigilante action, but only try and explain it."

I'm not sure what form of words would constitute a watertight justification of vigilantism, but that last paragraph comes close. Then, in a remarkable move, Mitra holds out 'Hindu' involvement in the Malegaon blasts as a sinister portent: "If the state does not shed its hypocrisy the alleged Malegaon plot may only be the beginning."

So from the illegitimacy of the notion of "Hindu terror" we've arrived at the prospect of chronic 'Hindu' violence if the state dares to apply to Hindus the police methods it routinely uses against Muslims.

The difference between Indians who respect the republic's constitution and the majoritarian right is this: constitutional democrats speak out against the police treatment of Sadhvi Pragnya Singh and Lt Col Purohit and the arrested students of Jamia Millia Islamia, because as citizens of this republic, this nation of laws, they deserve every protection the law has to offer. The Sangh Parivar demands these protections for Singh and Purohit alone, because they are Hindu. This is not a small difference: it's the difference between a civilized nation and a sectarian country, the difference, if you like, between India and Pakistan.

LIVING IN JAMIA NAGAR*

RAKHSHANDA JALIL

Living in the Jamia neighborhood has always been tough. The incidents of September, being dubbed the Battle of Batla House by the press, will only make it tougher. Biases, I suspect, will get sharper; discrimination more covert; and the gloves, I fear, will be off. A few years ago when I moved from Gulmohar Park, a tony locality in South Delhi, to the Jamia neighbourhood, little was I to know that I would be changing not merely a postal address and a landline telephone number but virtually exchanging one way of life for another.

The first rude shock came when I arranged my daughter's birthday party at our home. I sent detailed directions along with hand-made cards. My daughter, then nine, came home in tears because most of her friends had said they couldn't come. Perplexed by this sudden about-face, I called all the Mommies only to be told by most that they wouldn't be able to come 'there'. *Gulmohar Park ki baat alag thi; Jamia side ka hame koi idea nahi hai.* ("It was different in Gulmohar Park; we have no idea about the Jamia side.") I persevered by offering to draw maps, even volunteering to picking the kids from the nearest big landmark, the Holy Family Hospital. Yet, attendance slumped hugely from previous years. Thereafter, I learnt my lesson by organizing all such events at a conveniently located McDonalds.

That Delhi is ridiculously snobbish about addresses is a

---

* 'Why a Bias Against Jamia Nagar', *Times of India*, 29 September 2008.

well-known fact. But I have seen another colour creep into harmless idiosyncrasy when I disclose where I live. There is an imperceptible change. Some wonder aloud, "Oh, isn't it far?" Others look blank, "Jamia? Okhla? As in Industrial Area?" Still others walk away, wanting to have very little to do with someone who lives 'out there'. And out there where I live, several basic amenities are missing, that others in other parts of the city take for granted. Pizza boys from the nearby Domino's outlet in New Friends Colony do not venture out there. You can go blue in the face arguing that Jamia Nagar is closer to NFC as the crow flies than the most far-flung pocket of Sukhdev Vihar, but they stick to their 'rule'! Nor will Dry Cleaners who promise Free Home Delivery to the furthest block in Maharani Bagh come to your doorstep. The same applies to an assortment of chemists, florists and grocers. Believe me, I have argued, pleaded and threatened. Nothing works. They won't go 'out there'!

When I decided to spend less time commuting and move closer to my place of work, the Jamia Millia Islamia, I spent ten tortuous months looking for a house in nearby New Friends Colony, Sukhdev Vihar, and Sarita Vihar. Perfectly decent people in their perfectly middle-class drawing rooms froze us off when they saw our business card or heard our name. Others reneged on deals worked out through property dealers saying they wanted 'vegetarian tenants'! So, while a great many Muslims no doubt prefer to live in the Muslim-dominated neighbourhoods of Shaheen Bagh, Ghaffar Manzil, Noor Nagar, Zakir Nagar, Batla House, Abul Fazal Enclave et al for reasons of "security", many, I suspect, do so because they are left with no choice. They come in droves to live in some of these over-congested ill-equipped localities that are no better than urban slums because landlords in mixed neighbourhoods look upon them with suspicion and mistrust.

And what do the civic authorities do to tackle the chaos that unspools from these densely-packed warrens? They turn a blind eye. They drop an invisible *cordon sanitaire* between 'here' and 'out there', thus, for all practical purposes demarcating civil administration into two clearly-defined spaces: one neatly labeled "organized", the other falling under the clamorous category of "unorganized". Other epithets can be used for these two categories: authorized/unauthorized, clean/filthy, orderly/chaotic, spacious/cramped, cared for/uncared for, and so on. In the case of the outer fringes of Zakir Nagar that skirt the A Block of New Friends Colony, this contrast is especially stark: pockets of abysmal neglect exist cheek-by-jowl with oases of privilege. Yet it seldom causes so much as a raised eyebrow let alone any real degree of concern or introspection, either among the duly elected people's representatives or on the part of the bureaucrats who head our civic bodies.

While all of Delhi has a population of 11.72% Muslims, the Jamia Nagar neighbourhood is almost 98% Muslim; the Okhla ward alone has a population of 1,25,935. For this large body of people, there are branches of only three nationalized banks; the area having been declared a "Red Area", i.e. populated by "defaulters", few private banks even dream of venturing out here. The 8-km radius bogey for school admissions (mandated by the Delhi High Court) applies far more rigorously here than elsewhere, the mere address being enough to invoke the rulebook. There is no functioning MCD dispensary; local doctors refer all emergency cases to the nearby Holy Family Hospital (the nearest Government hospital is several km away). There are no Mother Dairy or Safal outlets (franchised by the Delhi Government and ubiquitous all over the city for their moderately priced fruits, vegetables and assorted perishables) for this sprawling area; a small booth vending milk products has been installed on the Jamia campus a few months ago on the vice-chancellor's personal initiative but that can barely cater to the students from nearby hostels. There are no Fair Price Shops, no government-funded training institutes to provide vocational training or any sort of facility to absorb the huge mass of school dropouts. In certain colonies such as Shaheen Bagh and Abul Fazal there is no drinking water; people buy water just as they would buy vegetables or groceries. Every morning you can see rickshaw pullers do a brisk business selling water of dubious vintage by the can-full.

What is happening in the Jamia neighbourhood can provide several useful lessons in urban morphology: (a) No community can take everything upon itself; it cannot be the *provider* and *user* of civic amenities, be it schools, universities, hospitals, ration shops, roads, electricity, water, group housing, sewage disposal or what-have-you; (b) While one cannot reverse the process of ghettoisation, one can certainly do much to integrate those who live in communally-charged ghettoes; and (c) If one fails or is seen to fail at all attempts at integration, one is creating conditions of urban unrest that have the potential to spill over.

LIVING A NIGHTMARE WITH REMARKABLE RESTRAINT*

RUMKI BASU

For the past two weeks, Jamia Millia Islamia has been in the news for all the wrong reasons. Even in my worst nightmare I did not imagine that I would walk up to my political science department one day to face mediapersons waiting to establish the identity of an alleged terrorist killed in the Jamia Nagar police encounter.

When we did check the records, it emerged that Atif Amin, the student in question, had taken admission in the human rights course this year as a day scholar, though he was yet to get an identity card made, having barely attended classes for a month.

The M.A. degree course in human rights like the M.A. course in public administration are unique courses — they are not offered anywhere in the capital except in our department. While our new student was dead, killed in the police encounter, our department's name was being flashed in the media, as if its only claim to fame was our association with this unknown 'terrorist'. Incidentally, in the Social Science School in Jamia, the political science department is the largest in terms of courses offered, student strength and number of faculty. Our department is an interesting experiment in multiculturalism—our students truly represent a microcosm of the 'idea' of India—coming as they do from almost two-thirds of Indian states and an equal divide in terms of Hindu/Muslim students.

* *The Subcontinent*, 5 October 2008.

The nightmare, I did realise, had just begun. Unfortunately, we had very little information on the alleged 'mastermind' whom some of my colleagues had barely seen for a month before he was declared dead. In the next few days, two students were arrested for their alleged involvement in the Sep 13 Delhi bomb blasts. They were students staying outside the campus, not even one was picked up from the student hostel in Jamia, a central university.

Most of my students from the human rights course looked terrified and completely lost in apprehension. More and more reports came in of students being 'picked up' by the police for questioning, leaving behind a trail of fear, mistrust, shock and disbelief on the campus. Many students who lived on rented accommodation in nearby areas of Jamia Nagar were simply asked to vacate rooms by their landlords for fear of police reprisals.

These 'homeless' students (about 2,500) had no option but to go home with no clue about their future options when they came back. Suddenly their futures seemed uncertain, their careers were at stake for reasons completely beyond their control or comprehension. An 80-year-old institution's secular and nationalist credentials were being virtually dragged in the mud and the future of its 12,000 students being held to ransom by the alleged terror links of a couple of students. Could anything be more unfair?

More than anybody, I am aware of the personal sagas of some of our poor and middle class students - their struggle to reach a Central University in Delhi from vernacular medium schools in villages and districts of far-flung states in India, had never been easy. They were students from Bihar, Uttar Pradesh, Jammu and Kashmir and the northeastern states, for whom Jamia seemed a truly 'happening', and therefore a preferred, academic destination in the last few years.

Jamia had seen unprecedented expansion in the past four years with the present vice chancellor's untiring efforts for mainstreaming the university and students were being offered core and optional courses in human rights, public administration, social work, education, management and journalism not offered anywhere in Delhi. 'Modernization' was the buzzword and the mood of the students upbeat. Jawaharlal Nehru University and Delhi University were obvious role models to follow and one could sense that our students were now ready for competition and exposure. Debate, dialogue and discuss - this is what universities need to do to change and transform mindsets since all ideas have to be ultimately introduced/defended/fought in the public sphere in all democracies.

It was at this point that terror struck. Terror can never be justified since no cause can be greater than the right to life—which is the only inviolable and non-negotiable natural human right. You cannot have any dialogue with terror: it strikes blindly and irrationally with fixed targets at times, at others with random. The Delhi blasts which hit the public at large indiscriminately have perhaps impacted civil society in exactly the same way as the 'post encounter aftermath' in Jamia - break spirits, polarise communities and suffocate chances of dialogue and peace. However, none of this did actually happen in Jamia itself, where the atmosphere on campus remained hurt but peaceful.

'Terrorism' was being debated, so were 'police encounters' and I was amazed by the maturity and objectivity of my students on arguments such as these. What emerged most strongly was that we must not communalise or valorise 'terrorism' in any way. There was a complete consensus also to protect the secular image of the institution and the fledging careers of our students - since both were equally at stake. There was continuous resentment however at the fact that the private behaviour of students outside the campus had to be justified/condemned/defended by Jamia Millia Islamia (a public institution)—the public-private divide somehow got obliterated in all that was happening on the Jamia campus.

We, as teachers of Jamia Millia Islamia, can only hope that this will pass and that the darkest hour is indeed before dawn. The fact that our students in the past two weeks have shown remarkable restraint and courage is our only ray of light at the end of this long tunnel—a result perhaps of the legacy of hope, faith and trust in the long standing secular traditions of Jamia - bequeathed to them over the years.

LIVING AND WORKING IN JAMIA*

LAKSHMI SUBRAMANIAN

The news of the Batla house encounter and its aftermath that included a media obsession with the Jamia Millia Islamia, an institution which I have the privilege of serving, came to me in Mabula Game reserve where I was taken as part of an academic trip organized by the University of Witwatersrand, Johannesburg. It was strangely unreal as I tried to come to grips with the kind of news that was filtering through Internet editions of newspapers and emails and to make sense of the insane presumptions that were being circulated about the neighborhood and the locality in which Jamia happens to be situated. From here it was but a step to reconfirm the oft-quoted connection between terror and Muslims, from self appointed media pundits to opposition leaders, the issue of complicity with the politics of terror was announced stridently and obsessively.

Trying to explain the furor to my colleagues in Wits, I realized just how far removed my own experiences were about not just the university but also the larger community it is congruent with. I live on campus and while it is admittedly a protected environment, I do have occasion to interact with my neighborhood fairly regularly even if it is mediated largely through the market. I believe it is important for me to share these quotidian experiences of working in the university and

* *The Hindu*, 26 October 2008.

living in the neighborhood just so as to be able to persuade more people to consider changing their blinkers.

I do not wish to go into the events that persuaded the Vice Chancellor to take what all of us believe was a courageous and compassionate step. What I do wish to talk about is the utter failure of our leaders to be able to provide the necessary succor to our youth, especially of the minority community whose fear and frustration at the damning label of a 'potential terrorist' is deeply demoralizing. Speaking to students of different backgrounds, I was struck by their bewilderment at the situation, when association with an institution and with a community into which they had been born seemed to suddenly disempower them completely. It is this quality of despair that smote me – for even in the short time I had experienced as a member of Jamia's teaching fraternity, I had been made conscious both of the enormous disadvantages that many of its students suffer and of the tranformative potential that they saw in being students of Jamia. Not all of them were exceptional or committed students – but what was important for me to register was that they saw the university as a space where they could engage with the experience of difference, with the potential of modernity without fear. And yet it was this very quality that the recent events seemed to undermine thanks to a specious political rhetoric, to a deeply communalized police force and to a sensation seeking media, which has lost its moral rationale.

My neighborhood is not by any means ideal. It is congested – pavements are non-existent, vehicular warfare on the streets keeps us on our toes and civic amenities are scarce especially in Batla House. It is, in terms of its residential patterns, not especially diverse and does bear the signs of being a ghettoized space. Having said that let me also put on record that in my experience of having lived in this area, I have never once felt out of place or threatened – on the contrary, I have had neighbors whom I do not even know, personally wishing me during festive occasions – ours, theirs under the circumstances lose all meaning. My domestic help keeps me vastly entertained and informed as he talks of his village and the ease and cordiality he shares with the larger Jat and Gujjar community. I am not suggesting for a minute that all these instances remove the ruptures that have cleaved Hindu-Muslim relations but nor am I prepared to gloss them over. I do not believe that malice and the politics of hate and misunderstanding should assume more political legitimacy than small instances of shared appreciation. I do believe that civil society and the political establishment sits up and start recognizing that instititutions like Jamia have in their small way traversed a considerable distance in nurturing a community of genuinely secular minded individuals who respond to difference and embrace pluralism as the only means of intellectual growth.

A COMMUNITY CAUGHT IN MYOPIC LENSES*

MEHER FATIMA HUSSAIN

Sitting in a faculty meeting at the Dr. K.R. Narayanan Centre for Dalit and Minorities Studies, Jamia Millia Islamia on 19 September, 2008 around 11 a.m., little did my colleagues and I imagine, in our wildest dreams, that the meeting would be disrupted and the university seized in a situation difficult to initially comprehend and that would later continue to resonate in the rest of our lives. While we were still discussing matters in the bona fide interests of our Centre when one my colleagues' mobile buzzed and she hastily made her exit only to return even faster to warn us that an ' encounter' was going on near Khalilullah Masjid in Batla House and for our own safety we should not venture out. As we tried to figure out the veracity of the information as well the incident, we could hear loud sirens making headways into the Batla House locality which is in the vicinity of our Centre. Within minutes there were even louder sirens as police vehicles zoomed in and out of Batla House. As situation seemed complicated, we took our position along the glass windows of the Noam Chomsky building to catch glimpses of things going on in the area.

I saw large gatherings of policemen making all possible moves to cordon off Jamia Nagar. Amidst them were ambitious media-men holding big cameras on their shoulders thrusting

* Written specially for this volume.

themselves into the prohibited locality. Their assistants laced with all modern gadgets and accessories were vying their best to facilitate the moves of their mentors. I was immensely surprised that how come the media had reached here so fast. Among those stranded were local residents and passer bys, cars, scooters, cycles, rickshaws and scooters. Soon big and small vans occupied the road as police personnel, para military forces with high-tech armaments alighted them to swarm the area. There was absolutely no dearth of well armed policemen in plain clothes moving in and out of Jamia Nagar. It was really moving to see little children cling on to the edges of cycle carriers looking helplessly as their distraught guardians struggled to abide by the policemen's prohibitory orders *"Aap Log Yahin Ruke, Aage Jaana Mana Hai"*(stop here and do not move further) . There was acute commotion since nobody had the slightest of the inkling that they would be caught in such mayhem. At around two in the afternoon I reached home and on the way saw deserted vehicles belonging to policemen and media parked along sides of the main road up to the Holy Family hospital. At home, I put on the television set to catch some details of the alleged 'encounter' and, not to my surprise, found all the news channels occupied in a frenzied race claiming they are 'the first' to bring details of the 'encounter' simultaneously bursting theories of 'terrorism' claiming involvement of Jamia students, without justifying the minimum eligibility of verification and proof. There was an armed operation conducted by the Special Cell of the Delhi Police in Flat number 108 in the building L-18 in Batla House area of Jamia Nagar in which Atif Amin and Sajid were shot dead while Police Inspector Mohan Chand Sharma underwent treatment at Holy Family hospital (later succumbed to his injuries). The media (as per police report) further claimed that two alleged 'terrorists' escaped during the operation. Some news channels even cautioned its audience to keep the doors and windows of the houses closed, not to entertain prospective tenants and strangers as they might be the alleged 'terrorists' who had escaped from Batla House and must be on a look out for asylum. Sitting comfortably in one's home one could hardly realize the problems that were being faced by young Muslim boys who by chance had reached Delhi from different cities and were looking for hotel rooms, a fact I came to realize after one of my relatives from Patna on a casual visit narrated a harrowing tale of finding a room on rent. On a broader canvas, little do the news channels realize that their irresponsible reportages not only put the image of Muslim community but also the destinies of young students of Jamia in peril.

Two Jamia students, Ziaur Rehman and Mohammed Shakeel, were arrested for their suspected involvement in terror activities. Thereafter, the sight of patrolling police with their mammoth vans hurled along Jamia's boundaries and into Jamia Nagar became a common feature. Classes in the university were resumed with the only difference that the attendance fell short for a couple of days but strength regained as efforts were made to reinstate confidence. Addressing a huge gathering of students collected at Ansari Auditorium on Jamia's campus, Vice Chancellor Professor Mushirul Hasan said "While the University will ensure that the students get fair justice, it has no intention of intervening with the judicial processes or impeding police enquiries." The session was meant to be off-limits for the press. Prof. Hasan further lashed out at the media saying, "The press has never been here to cover any of our events or to highlight the institution at the time of celebration. Then why are they here now? They should be in Bihar, Karnataka and Orissa looking for real stories." Prof. Hasan further said, contrary to what is being reported, there is absolutely no conspiracy happening here. "Yes, we were conspirators, but that was at the time of the freedom struggle. We are proud of having played the role then. That apart, I fail to understand why offering legal aid to the two students is being blown out of proportion. Legal representation is every citizen's right and I will not crucify my students unless proven guilty," Prof. Hasan announced amidst loud applause.

Later, speaking to the media at a press conference, Prof. Hasan tagged the arrests of the students as "isolated incidents" and appealed to the press to not "politicize it" and "protect the secular nature of the institution" as later reported in the

Hindustan Times dated 25 September 2008. Prof. Hasan praised the students for being disciplined and restrained even in the aftermath of the turmoil. Consequently, a peace march intended to instill confidence and solidarity among Jamia's fraternity was organized by the University's Outreach Programme wherein a large number of students and faculty members followed the Vice-Chancellor. This was further meant to reinstate confidence among the populace of Jamia Nagar.

Jamia's spokesperson Rakhshanda Jalil's article 'Why a bias against Jamia Nagar?' carried out in *The Times of India*, 29 September 2008, very succinctly encapsulates the indifference meted out to residents of Jamia Nagar by the administration and civic authorities which she observed would get further acute after the incident . She writes "living in Jamia neighbourhood has always been tough. The incidents of last week, being dubbed as the battle of Batla House by the press, will only make it tougher." Biases, she suspected, will get sharper and discrimination more covert. Her narration is close to the observation of Amratya Sen who uses the term 'unfreedom' to explain deprivation. Muslims would discover that the social facilities which give birth to economic opportunities and a sanguine outlook do not exist in adequate measure for them as they live in congested localities with lack of security. The fact of the matter is that they are more backward than any other community, therefore, they need to be helped to get out of the ghetto-like social environment in which a large number of them are obliged to live and function.

But such observations fail to catch the attention of administration and media who have only assisted in further worsening of the situation in Jamia Nagar. Shreya Roy Chowdhury in *The Times of India* dated 12 October 2008 revealed some of the difficulties which the students studying at Jamia suffered in the aftermath of the 'encounter'. Students were finding it extremely difficult to get accommodations. Still others feared studying late in the library will put them in risk of being "picked up by police" while returning to their homes or hostels. Rizwan Qaiser, Associate Professor in Jamia's Department of History and Culture said "the police and Muslims have always shared an uneasy relationship as their role in Mumbai and Gujarat has shown. Those hurts still rankle and added to them is the insult of having uniformed men patrolling the area, spreading more fear and anxiety among an already thoroughly rattled student community."

The Jamia Teachers' Solidarity Group worked its best to sensitize the issue and seek redressal of the grave atrocities committed in the name of "fighting terror". They compiled and released a Report in February 2009 titled *'Encounter' at Batla House: Unanswered Questions.* The Report points at serious procedural lapses in the whole operation by the police and the media. Some highlights in the report deserve mention namely... *The media reported just the police version of the story in a language and with visual aids that vastly heightened the atmosphere of fear. There were no follow-ups to ascertain whether the arrests and the encounters were genuine. After the arrests, the arrested persons simply disappeared from view. The media made no enquiries about their treatment in police custody, and whether the accused have been given the due protection of the law.....*

All these developments bring me closer to unravel another empirical report that very unambiguously uncovers the role of media *viz a viz* the minorities, particularly the Muslims. With the central objective being to understand whether media is sufficiently focused on the problems of the minorities in terms of social development, employment opportunities and opportunities for their participation in development and democracy, a study was conducted by Centre for Media Studies (CMS) and submitted to the National Commission for Minorities in December 2007. In the task, CMS media lab identified eight National News Channels, six Hindi and two English, that included Aaj Tak, CNN IBN, DD News, NDTV(India), NDTV 24x7, Sahara Samay, Star News and Zee News, and Prime Time news from 7-11 p.m. were monitored, recorded and analysed for a period of two months, i.e. April and May 2007. After the two months of monitoring and out of the 15,683 news stories that appeared in this period, it was found that out of these there were only 144 stories related to minorities, which accounts for merely 0.9 per cent of the news coverage.

During the period of review there were no international stories connected to Islam or Muslims. The Uttar Pradesh (UP) Assembly elections and the controversial release of CD by BJP (anti-Muslim contents) in UP which coincided with UP elections got about 30 per cent of the space. The remaining 70 per cent of coverage related top stories ranging from conflicts, controversies, development, issues and concern about status of Muslims and policy of terrorism. It was found that 'politicised' coverage got higher coverage in TV news than social change or basic issues or structural issues. The channels during the prime time devote less time to issues of development and process of change. Over all this is equally true in the case of minorities. Among the Muslim voices heard and seen were persons belonging to the category of opinion leaders and Party Politicos. For locating the story of minorities, the media have shown mostly stock pictures relating to Muslims in prayer, mosques, and women in Burqa (veil) or men in typical clothing. The finding in the report objectively bares the reality as to how much importance is being given to issues of minority concerns particularly the Muslims by the media. Since media is one of the most influential opinion makers and is a highly organized agency, it is therefore all the more necessary for the media to play a responsible and unbiased role in the greater interest of the nation. To borrow the expression of Lester Markel of *The New York Times,* "an informed opinion is a torch without a nation cannot find its way through the darkness."

Distorted news about Muslims, misinterpreted Muslim situations and twisted or misrepresented events have all led towards a climate of suspicion and mistrust, something which the Jamia Nagar is still reeling under. For the media the 'Batla House Encounter' might just be an ephemeral opportunity to boost their TRPs but for the overwhelming Muslim community residing in Jamia Nagar and for Jamia Millia Islamia, a university with immense secular credentials, this is just one more test when we need to prove our patriotism.

ALIENATED GENERATION*

MUSHIRUL HASAN

The extent to which our society is getting polarised along religious lines is very disturbing. If this is the state of affairs almost seven decades after independence, what might happen a few decades later? This is not the time to attribute responsibility to different parties or communities. This is a moment of self-reflection; of trying to find out what gives rise to this mindless violence.

The other very disquieting fact is how the electronic media and sections of the Hindi print media have taken upon themselves the responsibility of being the custodian of the nation's interest. The arrogance and intolerance in their coverage reflects a very ominous trend in the history of journalism. I have experienced this recently. The Jamia incident is not a big affair, it could have been easily sorted out, but it was turned into a campaign against a university. Our doors are open to non-Muslims; our teachers are drawn from all communities. Compare our record with that of other so-called secular universities where Muslims have limited access — Benaras Hindu University, Allahabad University, Delhi University itself — then what are we questioning?

A student at the London School of Economic (LSE) was nabbed very recently by the police — does it mean that the LSE has become a hotbed of terrorism? This is senseless. I think

* *Tehelka Magazine*, Vol. 5, Issue 40, Dated Oct 11, 2008.

we have to fight back. We have tolerated this nonsense for far too long. We should take on the media and demonstrate to the people that they are not trustworthy and are out to basically sensationalise events. Jamia Millia is being seen as the Muslim institution that it is not; it is a secular institution funded by the Central Government. The question of legal aid is not being looked at from the perspective of a teacher's responsibility to his students. As the head of the institution, I feel I have an obligation towards my students. And I am not using the taxpayer's money for it. But the real issue is of principle. If this had happened to a non-Muslim student, I would have done the same. I am also upholding the rule of law. Why have we forgotten the principle that says that an accused is innocent until proven guilty?

In the ultimate analysis, our society, which has gone through the Khalistan movement and experienced terrorism in the Northeast, must look at these incidents in a more cool-headed manner. Because you can't fight it by reacting in a hysterical manner. Also, our police is becoming more politicised and communalised. We haven't reoriented them into becoming the custodians of the secular values enshrined in the Constitution. Over the past 10 years, there has been a systematic pattern — Deoband University, an institution with a glorious record, has been targeted. So has Nadvat-ul-Ulema in Lucknow. Aligarh University has always been targeted, despite its being a modern institution with its doors open to all. Is there a pattern in this madness? We need to reflect on these issues. The alienation is very deep, and has to stop. But instead of supporting us, which would also mean supporting an institution committed to secular values, there are attempts to undermine our secular foundations.

And now we are dealing with a younger generation of Muslims. I believe in a liberal, eclectic and pluralist idea of Islam, but I suspect this vision will not be shared by those who are feeling insecure and excluded, socially and culturally. Why have the guilty in Gujarat not been punished? Why? Why? Why is the VHP and Bajrang Dal not banned for killing innocent Christians and desecrating their churches?

I regard myself, as do millions of others, as part of the edifice that is called India. The idea of India is my idea. There is no India without me, and I will not let that change. We have already taken certain steps to counter subversive ideas that might fracture our secular society. I appeal to civil society and the media to let us live in peace, and get on with our simple and innocent job — pursuit of knowledge. There is a limit to what one can tolerate. Nobody dare question our commitment to education, and our loyalty to the Indian Constitution.

IDEAS EXCHANGE*

INTERVIEW WITH MUSHIRUL HASAN

VANDITA MISHRA: Your academic council has expressed anguish over the kind of attention the University has been getting. What is it about the current situation that disturbs you the most?

All of us are appalled by the fact that the action of two or three students of the university has brought such disrepute to an institution which has consistently stood by all the values that are dear to all of us and which are enshrined in the Constitution. What is really amazing is that if a secular institution with a secular record can be targeted so easily, what will be the fate of non-secular institutions? I feel very, very distressed. I have no reason to believe that the character of the institution has changed or that its commitment has been diluted in any way. Absolutely not. We are completely secular. We don't even ask our students about their religion in their application form. There is no preference for Muslims per se and a large number of the teachers are non-Muslims. A large number of students who are non-Muslims have never experienced any sense of discrimination.

The role of the media has also been distressing. We all value freedom of expression but I think the way the electronic media, especially, has behaved is extremely alarming. Very often, there

* 'Ideas Exchange' series in *The Indian Express*, 5 October 2008. The longer text is available *on* www.expressindia.com.

is no story and yet a story is invented. In this particular instance, OB vans landed up in large numbers and virtually instigated students to say something. It's as though you expect a Muslim student to say something that would project the image of 'the Muslim'. And when that Muslim makes a liberal or a secular statement, that statement will seldom find mention because that statement is of no interest. A liberal and secular Muslim is not someone you can sell in the market.

Over the last few years, Jamia has promoted a liberal, modem and enlightened agenda. Oxford, Cambridge, Princeton and Harvard come to us with MoUs. But that is not something that will ever get reported. We name our buildings after individuals. Why? Because dead or alive we want to tell the world that Noam Chomsky is part of our intellectual legacy, that Nehru, Gandhi and Jamnalal Bajaj are as much a part of our legacy as Mohammad All or Syed Ahmad Khan. They are all secular figures. It's been a Herculean effort to do this kind of thing. To see how easily, quickly, so ruthlessly and so crudely things have been twisted and distorted is distressing. In the last three years, Jamia has been the venue of at least seven conferences organised against Islamic terrorism. That people should even raise a question about our credentials is infuriating.

VANDITA MISHRA: Why did you decide to offer legal aid to the accused students?

I have no doubt that what I did was absolutely right. The head of an institution is like a parent. Just as we would provide medical or travel aid to students, we would provide legal aid too. What is so wrong about it? This is a constitutional right that every citizen is entitled to in a free society. We are not defending the students. There is a difference between providing legal aid and defending them. I don't know these students. But our position is clear: we will provide access to legal aid. Thereafter, they are on their own. We are not going to defend them or go unnecessarily out our way to say they're innocent.

COOMI KAPOOR: The criticism of your actions is that it sets a precedent. What if this precedent were to be applied to other universities with a high degree of criminality?

We're not defending criminality. There is a specific context in which this whole thing has happened. This is the case of two students who haven't been proven guilty as yet. It's as simple as that. If they are proven guilty, there is no question of any kind of help-moral, legal or financial.

VANDITA MISHRA: You said the university has held conferences to discuss terror. Has any discussion touched upon the issue that confronts us now-that of homegrown terror involving the urban, educated Muslim?

Of course, we have. We know there is homegrown terrorism. How will you address it? You have to isolate those who are out to undermine the democratic-secular edifice of our society. But how do you do it? You don't do it by a legislation such as POTA. You devise effective legislation, the kind of legislation that would counter not only Muslim terrorism but the terror unleashed by the VHP, by the BJP as is evident from what has happened in Malegaon and in Karnataka. What is happening is a national problem and has to be dealt with in the larger framework of keeping our social fabric intact. You can't isolate these things. The blast in Delhi's Mehrauli hit headlines but when a similar one took place in Malegaon, it was a small story. This does not send out the right message.

It does not seem as if we, as a nation, are collectively engaged in fighting terrorism. It suggests that you only associate terrorism with Muslims. I was speaking at a conference on Gandhi and Khan Abdul Ghaffar Khan. A whole auditorium can be filled up with books on Islam and violence but what about Islam and non-violence? What about Ghaffar Khan? Does he not exist or is he of no consequence because he does not fit the stereotype that some people wish to create and perpetuate about an entire community?

SUMAN K. JHA: Jamia has a street named after Arjun Singh. How would you defend his being given this privilege in the university, which he is said to be using to score political brownie points?

I don't think it is fair to draw Mr Arjun Singh into this controversy because apart from vindicating the position of the academic council, he has no role to play. He has been tremendously supportive to the institution and I think the entire

Jamia fraternity is extremely grateful to him for what he has done, having sensed the fact that Jamia has been the victim of neglect for the last 55 years. So if you want to grudge Arjun Singh for extending financial support, which was not out of proportion and was well within the rules, then I can't , help that, but please don't associate his name with this controversy.

To suggest that he is using this, as some people said in a television interview, for the election is completely preposterous. Yes, we have named a building and a street after him. And I wish there were more buildings that I could name after him. He very strongly opposed the idea of a building being named after him and I think some of my colleagues persuaded him to accept it. He has done more for the institution than anybody else, and yes, may be the next building, a bigger one, can be called 'Arjun Singh'.

SEEMA CHISHTI: Some years ago, when you took a stand against banning Salman Rushdie's Satanic Verses, you were targeted by hotheaded people who happened to be Muslim. Now you have some people in the BJP accusing you of supporting terrorists. How has this affected you?

The opposition of certain sections did not deter me from pursuing my intellectual agenda because I have no political interests. There has been no change in my understanding of the dangers inherent in fundamentalist positions, whether they are political or religious. I believed then, as I believe now, that an enlightened hDeral and secular position is a position that both the majority and the minority communities must pursue. It's been a difficult journey in many ways but then I suppose, as people say, one has to pay a price for taking positions.

SHRAVAN SEN: Would you say your university is being victimized just because it's a minority institution?

We are not a minority institution. We're created by an Act of Parliament, we're accountable to Parliament, we have no reservations for minorities, for Muslims. We have the usual reservations for SC/STs and OBCs. If you want to see how a genuinely secular and liberal institution works in India, come to Jamia.

PRANAB DHAL SAMANTA: What practical measures, if

any, are you now taking to prevent or to reduce the chances of such incidents being linked to your institution?

The day after the incident, I addressed students in our auditorium and said the answer to this is to be more secular, to be more liberal in your outlook, to be more enlightened in your perspective. The next day we organised a peace march. We had a big demonstration for peace and against violence and terrorism. It is being made out as if for the last 60 years, Jamia has been the hotbed of 'sedition'. The assumption is quite ridiculous because nothing has ever happened on the campus.

What administrative step can I take? I can only do what I've been doing. Who in his right sense would not condemn terror and terrorism or violence of any sort? We are not inciting students. Our job is to make sure that students remain calm, as we've done in the context of this incident. But the role of a teacher is a very limited one because terrorists are produced, not by universities, but by the society that nurtures the students.

C. JAYANTI: Why doesn't the liberal Muslim intelligentsia speak out more often against terrorism so that in people's minds, Islam isn't equated with it?

You probably don't hear those voices.

When a Muslim makes a liberal or a secular statement, it will seldom find mention because it is of no interest. A liberal and secular Muslim is not someone you can sell in the market because you don't want to hear those voices. The media doesn't represent those voices because the media is only interested in strident voices. They are not interested in the sane, liberal, rational voices. Look at the social science literature produced over the last 60 years and look at the Muslim writers — although they would be upset with this categorisation — Irfan Habib, Shahid Amin or scores of others. Are these not liberal voices? What do you want us to do? Stand on a terrace and announce that we are liberal Muslims and that we want to proclaim our loyalty to the nation? This is an expectation which, I'm afraid, we cannot fulfill. What have the Muslims done in 60-odd years which goes against the interests of the nation? Why don't you ask the Sikhs to proclaim their loyalty? I'm sorry I'm being very blunt. Who spoke out on Gujarat? You all condemn the Muslim communalist and I join you in condemning the Muslim communalist. But I condemn the Hindu communalist as well, which you all don't. What should the liberal Muslims do? The fact that they are still liberals in this sort of situation — caught between the devil and the deep sea — you should give them a Padma award.

You cannot play a constructive role by castigating your community. This is bad politics. You have to be sympathetic to the concerns and aspirations of the community because 150 million Muslims are not all mad, are they? If they have grievances you have to understand them.

SHWETA DUTTA: How negative an impact has the constant 'othering' of the Muslim community had on young people of the community?

Young Muslims have no cultural baggage of Partition or '47. They were born and brought up in a democratic, secular India and have a stake in the system-as much a stake as anybody else. Yet, there is this distancing, this 'othering'.

The problem today, sadly, is that the left forces have weakened, socialist elements have disappeared and the centrist forces are susceptible to communalism. This is a problem more essentially in the North. It is not a problem in the South where the barriers that existed in those societies have been overcome. Which is why, the Muslims are better integrated in those societies. Kerala, Karnataka or Tamil Nadu are models of a multi-religious and multicultural society. There the Muslims are a little more advanced and a little more forward-looking than in the North or even in Bengal.

NEHA SINHA: Many young Muslims in Delhi's Jamia Nagar where the alleged terrorists lived, feel that they face a forced ghettoisation. They don't get houses, they don't get credit cards. Do you think that to challenge stereotypes in young people from the community and young people from outside the community we need curricular changes?

I think at this juncture the main task should be to restore the confidence of the people in the system. I think it's extremely important that they should not feel alienated. I think it's very sad that some Muslim students have been evicted from accommodations because the entire university is being dubbed as the hotbed of terrorism. I think it is important to stress how life goes on norma1ly, how despite the provocation, the situation is extremely peaceful.

I have said to people in government that there is a larger questi6n that needs to be addressed: that of providing basic civic amenities to these areas'. If you visit these areas you will be appalled by the conditions in which people live. It is very close to some posh Delhi enclaves but there is no clean water, no sewage, no sanitation, no Mother Dairy. The Delhi government has to defuse the tension in the area and stop the alienation which is very, very deep rooted there.

PRESERVING OUR SECULAR INHERITANCE*

INTERVIEW OF MUSHIRUL HASAN BY PURNIMA S. TRIPATHI

Everyone was surprised by your announcement that the university would provide legal aid to students arrested for their alleged involvement in the bomb blasts. What made you take this stand?

These are only charges at the moment. Our jurisprudence dictates that one is innocent until proven guilty. This was my personal decision because I felt as a teacher and as the head of an institution, it was my moral responsibility. After all, is the teacher not considered the *mai-baap* [mother-father] of his students? I was only trying to calm nerves on the campus and assure my students and the faculty that nobody is denied his or her fundamental rights in this country. I have nothing to say on the encounter; it is outside my brief. But I had to come into the picture because three of our students were involved. I was concerned about its impact on the campus.

How would you justify your stand, all the more because Jamia is a Central university and the BJP says you are spending taxpayers' money to help terrorists?

I owe no explanation or justification to anybody. Those who know me c aware of my credentials will under stand my decision. As for the critic from the BJP, I take it as a certificate

* *Frontline*, October 2008

my "good conduct". Any words of appreciation from the BJP, in fact, would embarrass me. Their criticism is pr that I am on the right track.

As for spending taxpayers' me this is not true. The funds are being contributed by the teachers voluntarily. There is a committee for this purpose. Besides, we have a students' aid fund from which we regularly help students in situations like medical emergencies. We have spent from this fund for arranging bails in the case of an incident of violence in which 40 students were arrested. So this is not something we have done for the first time.

But here the charges are of being involved in terrorist activities.

That is still to be proved. I took the decision to foil the attempt by a section of the political parties and the media to damage the university's image. Just because a couple of students have been implicated in cases, it does not make the entire university a nerve centre of terrorist activity. This vicarious attempt by a section to discredit the independent, pluralist and secular credentials of the university is unfortunate and it was to defeat this campaign that I took this stand. I owe no explanation for my conduct to anybody.

After I decided, I merely informed the HRD Minister, UGC [University Grants Commission] Chairman, the Secretary and the Joint Secretary concerned. They are not obliged either to agree or disagree with me. My only intention is to defend and preserve the secular inheritance of our university and calm nerves.

As for the students being accused of involvement in terrorist activities, let them be proven guilty first. The law of the land says that you are innocent until proven guilty. If they are proven guilty and convicted, good, bad and sad. They would deserve their punishment. But if they are exonerated, then also it is fine, no big cause for jubilation. I can assure you that if ever any of my students were found expressing solidarity with terrorism anywhere, I would be the first person to quit. The spirit of the university must not be compromised or tarnished by anyone whatsoever.

What is the impact of the incident on the campus?

Except for the first few days of nervous tension, the campus has been a model of exemplary behaviour. We had a massive peace march in which 9,000-10,000 students participated. But yes, there is a sense of insecurity among students, which is true for both Hindu and Muslim students. Landlords in the neighbouring areas are asking our students to vacate their houses; the very sight of the police makes the students nervous.

The university administration, however, is trying to instill a sense of security among the students. We asked the government to remove the police from the campus immediately afterwards. We are also trying to solve the hostel problem; we are building a new hostel for about 1,500 students, which should be ready in six to eight months.

The biggest assurance, however, has been the fact that the faculty is solidly behind the administration and has been instrumental in restoring the faith and confidence of the locality in the honour and secular image of the university. They also feel that the impeccable reputation of the university cannot be damaged by isolated nonevents like this.

Has the incident affected the placement process?

Unfortunately yes, some of our students have been asked embarrassing questions. Though this carmot be helped at the moment, I hope, with the passage of time, this will stop.

Does it hurt you that despite having such an impeccable reputation you have to stand up and declare your secular credentials?

Well, this cannot be helped, I guess. But I do hope that this phase is short-lived, as the problems in Punjab were. I do hope that this is a passing phase and will pass by without much damage to our great institution.

The BJP has criticized you. Has any political party expressed solidarity with you?

I don't want to be involved in political battles. I am keen that political parties should not jump into the fray on this issue. We have not had any public meeting addressed by any political leader on the campus; we have not had any politicians visiting us.

I wanted no political *tamasha* (show), no rhetoric, no speeches, nothing. The ABVP [Akhil Bharatiya Vidyarthi Parishad, the student wing of the BJP] tried to enter the campus shouting slogans, but they were stopped outside.

Are you convinced that your students are not guilty? Do you check their antecedents at the time of admission?

What sort of an antecedent can a 19- or 20-year-old have? They mostly come from poor families, from far-off areas. As for these two [students], I can't say until the investigations are complete. It may or may not be true, they might have been misled, brain-washed by vested interests. I cannot vouch for that. But it is not possible for us to check the antecedents of all students. We have no such agency at our disposal. In fact, we have no column in our admission forms even to identify students as Hindus or Muslims.

NOTES ON CONTRIBUTORS

MARTHA NUSSBAUM is Ernst Freund Distinguished Service Professor of Law and Ethics at the University of Chicago, a chair that includes appointments in the Philosophy Department, the Law School, and the Divinity School. She has previously taught at Harvard and Brown. She has written, among others, *Frontiers of Justice: Disability, Nationality, Species Membership* and *The Clash Within: Democracy, Religious Violence, and India's Future.*

GITHA HARIHARAN winner of the Commonwealth Writers Prize for Best First Fiction in1993for her first first novel, *The Thousand Faces of Night*. Since then, she has written *The Ghosts of Vasu Master* (1994), *When Dreams Travel* (1999), *In Times of Siege* (2003), and the new *Fugitive Histories* (2009). A collection of highly acclaimed short stories, *The Art of Dying*, was published in 1993, and a book of stories for children, *The Winning Team*, in 2004. She has also edited a volume of stories in English translation from four major South Indian languages, *A Southern Harvest* (1993); and co-edited a collection of stories for children, *Sorry, Best Friend!* (1997). She has been Writer-in Residence at the Jamia Millia Islamia. Her latest book is *Fugitive Histories*.

SUDHIR CHANDRA has previously taught History at the Jamia Millia Islamia. He writes a regular column for the Hindi newspaper *Jansatta* and has authored *The Oppressive Present: Literature and Social Consciousness in Colonial India* (OUP, 1992), *Enslaved Daughters: Colonialism, Law and Women's Rights* (OUP, 1998), *Continuing Dilemmas: Understanding Social Consciousness* (Tulika, 2002), and *Hindu, Hindutva, Hindustan* (in Hindi, Rajkamal Prakashan, 2003). He is currently working on Gandhi's last days and conversion to Christianity in British India.

AMEENA KAZI ANSARI teaches in the Department of English, Jamia Millia Islamia. She has worked and published in the areas of literary translation and postcolonial literature. Apart from articles and reviews, she has published *English-Canadian Literary Canon: Emergence and Development* (2004), *Partitions* (2006), a translation of Kamleshwar's award-winning Hindi novel, *Kitne Pakistan*, and co-edited *Translation/ Representation* (2007). She has also visited the USA as a nominee of the US Government's International Visitors Leadership Program (IVLP) in 2007.

AYESHA SIDDIQA is an independent security analyst and strategic affairs columnist of Pakistan. She received her doctorate from King's College, London in 1996 and has worked on issues of military technology, defense decision-making, nuclear deterrence, arms procurement, arms production to civil-military relations in South Asia. Her books include